BORED
OF
LUNCH

The Healthy Air Fryer Book

BORED
OF
LUNCH

The Healthy Air Fryer Book

NATHAN ANTHONY

CONTENTS

Welcome

Welcome to my second Bored of Lunch book. Wow! That sounds so surreal saying that. If you are new to Bored of Lunch – you are very welcome! I think you are going to love these books.

For those who don't already know me, my name is Nathan, and I'm not a chef and I don't work in the food industry. I am a busy home cook with a full-time job so the recipes in this book, like the recipes I post online, are tailored for those who want delicious healthy food that isn't going to take them ages to make.

I published my first book, *The Healthy Slow Cooker Book* in January 2023 and its aim was to encourage people to embrace this amazing time-saving kitchen gadget to enable you to make healthy (or sometimes just *healthier*) food. Well, now it's the air fryer's turn.

For anyone who already follows me online, you know how much I love my air fryer. Not only does it make it possible to create lower-fat versions of your everyday favourites, it is also much faster than a conventional oven and (my favourite part) only uses a fraction of the electricity, making it a much more cost-effective way to cook.

Now, I'm not a dietitian, and I don't come from a fitness background but I do count my calories, just so I can keep an eye on what I'm eating over a week. With this in mind, I have included the calories for all of the recipes for anyone else who finds it useful to track. That's not to say that all the recipes in this book are super 'lean' or 'low calorie'. Just like my first book, there is a full range of recipes in here to help you manage a healthy balance of nutritious food that also makes you feel satisfied.

On the pages that follow you can expect recipes to recreate some of your favourite takeaways in the Fakeaways chapter (pages 120–149), ideas for midweek dishes mastered in a low-fat way in Weekday Dinners (pages 88–119) and loads of ideas for Speedy Lunches (pages 48-87). Add to that, chapters full of starters and snacks, sides and some delicious sweet treats, I know you'll find food in here for any occasion, no matter who you're cooking for. I hope you enjoy these dishes, and please do share them with me on social media. I love seeing people recreate my recipes at home.

Love,
Nathan

AIR FRYER INSTRUCTIONS

In my opinion an air fryer is one of the best kitchen gadgets you can have in your arsenal, especially if you are counting calories or trying to slim down. These brilliant machines reduce the need for oil when frying food to merely a small spray, because they cook using hot air instead, but they still give that awesome crispiness that we all desire from fried food. The compact space through which the heat is blasted cooks the food quicker, too. One of the additional benefits of an air fryer beyond speed is how cost-effective they are, because they use much less energy than your traditional oven, thus saving you time and money.

Every air fryer is slightly different, and even when different machines are set to the same temperature some will cook things quicker than others, in my experience, so get to know your own machine. You might need to slightly alter the timings set out in this book by 1–2 minutes, but you will pick this up quickly. I now know my air fryer like the back of my hand.

Air fryers that have a basket or drawer tend to perform better than those with an oven-like door. Some machines rotate, which I wouldn't recommend as this will remove any coating you have applied – such as breadcrumbs on chicken, for example. If you have a drawer-based air fryer, you can give it a gentle shake during cooking to ensure nothing sticks, then you will get a very even cook across all the contents.

The air fryer that I recommend for roughly four portions of food would be a 4-6 quart machine – mine has two drawers so I can separate, for example, fries from chicken, which is perfect. There are so many types of air fryers to choose from, the one I recommend has a handle on the drawer. Some air fryers have shelves and look like mini ovens, but I have found they are pretty much just an oven and don't give the same crispy results.

AIR FRYER INSTRUCTIONS

AIR FRYER COOKING GUIDE

This table gives the perfect guide to cooking in your air fryer. Some of the cooking times may vary and might need to be adjusted based on the weight of products and your air fryer, so this is just a general guide (see page 8). The sizes used are standard supermarket product averages.

FISH	Cod fillets	10–12 minutes	400°F
	Scallops	7–8 minutes *turn halfway through*	400°F
	Tuna steak	12 minutes	350°F
	Salmon	12–14 minutes	350°F
	Shrimp	7 minutes	350°F
VEG	Potatoes (chopped into small chunks)	20 minutes	400°F
	Potato (whole)	45 minutes	400°F
	Sweet potato (whole)	35 minutes	400°F
	Kale	6 minutes	400°F
	Sliced mushrooms	7 minutes	400°F
	Tomatoes	6 minutes	335°F
	Broccoli florets	8 minutes	400°F
	Broccolini	5–6 minutes	400°F
	Asparagus	6 minutes	400°F

MEAT	Whole chicken	1 hour 15 minutes	375°F
	Chicken breasts	17–18 minutes	375°F
	Chicken drumsticks	22 minutes	200°C
	Chicken tenders	11 minutes	200°C
	Chicken wings	15–22 minutes	200°C
	Sausages	15 minutes	200°C
	Bacon slices	8–9 minutes	375°F
	Beef burgers	12–15 minutes	375°F
	Pork chops	10 minutes	200°C
	Steak	8–15 minutes *adjust on preference*	200°C
	Rack of lamb	22–25 minutes	200°C
	Lamb chops	11 minutes	200°C
FROZEN FOODS	Chicken tenders	14 minutes	375°F
	Chicken nuggets	10–11 minutes	200°C
	Fries (thin-cut)	15 minutes	375°F
	Fries (thick-cut)	18–20 minutes	375°F
	Onion rings	9 minutes	375°F
	Fish fillets	12–14 minutes	200°C
	Spring rolls	12–14 minutes	375°F
	Pizza	10–12 minutes	375°F
	Hash browns	12 minutes	200°C

PANTRY ESSENTIALS

Here I've included a list of some of my most-used ingredients that I try to have on hand so that I can create tasty, healthy food at home. It's not an exhaustive list and you definitely don't need to go out and buy them all at once. These are just some of the staples I aim to have in stock and recommend that you do too.

I don't come from a food or fitness background but I do believe in tracking calories to suit your nutritional needs and goals. There are lots of apps online that will recommend your ideal calorie count based on your height and weight. I've included the calorie count of these recipes to help them fit into your lifestyle, whether you're trying to reduce or maintain your calorie target for the day.

FOR FLAVOUR

- Dried herbs – in particular oregano, basil, thyme, rosemary, coriander
- Paprika, chilli flakes, garlic powder, onion powder, chilli powder
- Salt and pepper

FOR FAKEAWAY RECIPES

- Soy sauce, hoisin sauce, honey, rice vinegar, tins of coconut milk, sriracha, peanut butter
- Garlic and ginger – you can use fresh, dried, frozen or jars of chopped ginger/garlic

SAUCE ESSENTIALS

- Stock cubes – veg, chicken and beef
- Cornstarch to help you thicken a sauce and coat your meats
- Tins of chopped tomatoes or marinara sauce
- Tomato purée
- Worcestershire sauce

TO PAIR WITH YOUR AIR-FRIED FOODS

- Rice
- Couscous
- Pasta
- Potatoes of all kinds – you can cook these in the air fryer too
- Low-calorie spray

FRESH FOR EVEN MORE FLAVOUR

- Coriander leaves
- Basil leaves
- Rosemary
- Lemon and lime
- White onions

STARTERS & SNACKS

Also known as crab rangoons, these are actually an invention of American Chinese cuisine, but I first came across them at a friend's New Year's Eve party and fell in love. I knew I had to try my own version in the air fryer and this is the result.

CRAB PUFFS

MAKES 20–25

5 ¼ oz fresh white crab meat
6 oz reduced-fat cream
   cheese
1 tsp black pepper
pinch of chopped dill
1 tbsp soy sauce
20–25 wonton wrappers
   (depending on how well
   you fill them)

a little water or 1 beaten egg,
   for sealing
white sesame seeds, for
   sprinkling
soy sauce and sweet chilli
   sauce, for dipping

1 In a bowl combine the crab, cream cheese, pepper, dill and soy sauce.

2 Lay out your wonton wrappers and add roughly ½ tablespoon of the crab mixture to the middle of each wrapper. Using your fingers, wet the edges of the wrappers and crimp together into a parcel, pressing them together with good pressure so they seal well.

3 Once sealed, either brush all over with a little water or glaze with beaten egg, then sprinkle with the sesame seeds.

4 Air-fry at 335°F for 7 minutes.

5 Serve with soy sauce and sweet chilli sauce for dipping.

STARTERS & SNACKS

EACH
140
CALORIES

I can never resist arancini if I see them on a menu, and they're even better if they're made with 'nduja or chorizo. You can either use leftover rice for these or cook some fresh, but if you do this, I find it's better to cook it the night before, as it sticks together better the next day – just simmer the rice in chicken stock, drain and cool completely before popping in the fridge overnight.

'NDUJA-STUFFED ARANCINI BALLS

**MAKES ROUGHLY
16 BALLS**

2 cups cooked risotto rice, such as arborio
3 eggs
3 tbsp butter, melted
2 tbsp grated parmesan
1 cup mozzarella

1 ¼ cup panko breadcrumbs
1 tbsp Italian seasoning
½ lb 'nduja or cooked chorizo
low-calorie oil spray
salt and pepper, to taste

1 Take the rice out of the fridge and allow to come to room temperature.

2 Beat 2 of the eggs in a large bowl, add the melted butter, parmesan and most of the mozzarella and season to taste.

3 Combine the breadcrumbs and Italian seasoning in another bowl.

4 Take a tablespoon of the rice mixture and press it together into a ball, then flatten the ball and put a piece of 'nduja or chorizo in the middle along with some of the egg and mozzarella mix. Enclose the filling with the rice and roll it into a ball. You might need to wet your hands for this.

I use light or reduced-fat mozzarella but just use whatever you can find.

5 Beat the remaining egg in a bowl and dip in the rice ball, then roll it in the breadcrumbs to coat. Repeat with the remaining mixture.

6 Spray the rice balls well with a low-calorie spray and cook in an air fryer preheated to 375°F for 8 minutes.

When you think of spring rolls, veggie or duck fillings usually come to mind, but these are a little bit different. Honey, chilli and garlic is always a sensational combo, and these are incredible. I tend to serve them with a sweet chilli dip.

HONEY, GARLIC & CHILLI CHICKEN SPRING ROLLS

MAKES 12

3 cups cooked chicken, shredded
4 garlic cloves, crushed
½ tsp chilli flakes
6 tbsp honey
1 tbsp sriracha

1 packet of filo pastry sheets (or less, depending on how big you want the rolls)
low-calorie oil spray
sliced spring onions, to garnish

1 Mix the shredded chicken, garlic, chilli, honey and sriracha. Divide each sheet of filo pastry into 4 squares, then, taking one square at a time, place a spoonful of the mixture in the middle, fold 2 of the corners in and roll like you are making a wrap for lunch. Keep the other squares of filo covered with a damp cloth to stop them drying out.

2 When all the rolls are prepared, spray them with the oil, coating them really well, and cook in the air fryer at 375°F for 8 minutes. Turn them halfway through the cooking time and spray with more oil if required.

3 Garnish with the spring onions and let them cool for a few minutes before eating as the filling will be hot.

This is such a simple recipe, and it's perfect if you are catering for friends or just making snacks at home for yourself. I am low-key obsessed with halloumi to the point that it's getting out of control! I buy a block every week and the struggle for it to stay in the fridge for more than a day is real.

HALLOUMI FRIES
WITH A SWEET & SPICY MAYO

SERVES 3

8.8 oz block of halloumi
1 egg
1 ½ cups cornflakes, crushed
1 tbsp paprika
low-calorie oil spray
fresh coriander, to garnish

Spicy mayo
3 tbsp light mayo
3 tbsp sriracha
1 tbsp sweet chilli sauce
½ tsp paprika

1 Cut the halloumi into fries. Beat the egg in one bowl, then add the crushed cornflakes to another bowl and mix in the paprika.

2 Coat the halloumi fries in the low-calorie oil, then dip them first into the beaten egg, shaking off any excess, then into the cornflakes to coat.

3 Cook in the air fryer at 350°F for 10 minutes.

4 While the halloumi fries are cooking, combine all the spicy mayo ingredients in a bowl and serve with the cooked fries.

5 Top with some fresh coriander.

I love the texture of a crumpet, and this easy tear 'n' share is a perfect alternative when you are *this* close to ordering a pizza on a Tuesday night. Hopefully this cheesy, garlicky number will satisfy any greasy pizza cravings and save you money at the same time. I've suggested this serves 3–4, but it will do just as well for two hungry people.

CHEESY GARLIC CRUMPET TEAR 'N' SHARE

SERVES 4

6 garlic cloves, crushed
½ cup softened butter
pinch of sea salt
handful of freshly chopped
    parsley

8 crumpets (or 4 English
    muffins, halved lengthwise)
1 cup grated mozzarella
    cheese (preferably
    reduced-fat)

1 In a bowl, combine the garlic, butter, salt and parsley.

2 Spread all of the crumpets with the garlic butter. Top half of the crumpets with a little mozzarella, then sandwich together with the remaining crumpets. Cut the crumpets in half and scatter in an ovenproof dish, there is no art to it so organise in whatever way you like.

3 Top with the remaining mozzarella.

4 Air-fry at 350°F for 8–9 minutes, then tear and share the life out of it!

I am not sure how the Italian nation will feel about me taking one of their most-loved pastas and pairing it with chicken wings, but these are sensational. *Aglio e olio* is one of my all-time favourite pasta sauces, so pairing this gorgeous dressing with crispy chicken wings is a match like no other.

AGLIO E OLIO CHICKEN WINGS

SERVES 4

15–20 chicken wings, skin on
4 tbsp olive oil
1 tsp garlic powder
1 red chilli, chopped

2 garlic cloves, crushed
good handful of fresh basil
2 tbsp grated parmesan
salt and pepper, to taste

1 Pat dry the chicken wings with some paper towels, then coat them in 1 tablespoon of the oil and sprinkle with the garlic powder. Air-fry at 400°F for 17 minutes. Halfway through, turn over or shake so you get an even cook.

2 Just before the chicken has finished cooking, heat the rest of the oil in a pan, add the chilli and crushed garlic, season with salt and pepper and cook for 1–2 minutes.

3 Chilli oil should be stirred through all the ingredients.

STARTERS & SNACKS

Now I know I've put this in the sharing section, but I find these very hard to share. My advice is, feel free to make them for yourself and enjoy alone. I use shop-bought ravioli here, so they really couldn't be any easier to make.

OOZING RAVIOLI BITES

SERVES 3

1 ¼ cup breadcrumbs
½ cup parmesan, grated,
 plus extra to serve
pinch of salt
9 oz packet of ravioli

1 egg, beaten
handful of basil, chopped
tomato-based dipping sauce
 (marinara is perfect),
 to serve

1 Combine the breadcrumbs, parmesan and salt in a bowl.

2 Dip the ravioli into the beaten egg, shaking off any excess, then roll it in the crumb mix to coat.

3 Cook in the air fryer at 375°F for 10 minutes.

4 Sprinkle with a little parmesan and chopped basil to add some punchy flavours and serve with the tomato sauce.

Tortilla wraps can be a great replacement for all sorts of ingredients if you're trying to reduce calories. Here, I'm using them in place of pastry to make low-fat sausage rolls. This recipe uses low-fat sausages, too, but I promise with the right seasoning you won't be compromising on taste. Whether you're looking to cut down on calories or you're just after something a little lighter, these will satisfy even the most aggressive sausage-roll craving. Pair with your dip of choice.

SAUSAGE ROLL BITES

MAKES 10 BITES

6 low-fat sausages
1 tsp dried sage
1 tsp dried thyme
2 sprigs of rosemary,
   chopped

1 tortilla wrap
1 egg, beaten
sesame seeds, for sprinkling
salt, to taste

1 Remove the sausages from their skins, or if you prefer just squish them in a bowl with a fork. Mix in the sage, thyme and rosemary, then season with salt.

2 Spread the mixture onto one large wrap but on one side leave a thumb-sized gap for some egg wash. Form into a long roll, then cut into 8-10 small sausage rolls, depending on how thick you like them.

3 Brush the sausage rolls with beaten egg and sprinkle with sesame seeds.

4 Air-fry at 400°F for 11 minutes.

Zucchini or courgette, call them what you want, this is such a tasty recipe and low in calories. Crispy, crunchy, and with a beautiful taste from the parmesan, these make an absolutely delicious snack, but work well as a side, too, if you're trying to get more veg into your meals. You can serve these with some tzatziki on the side, or your favourite cupboard sauce might just be all you need.

ZUCCHINI FRIES

SERVES 3

3 zucchini
½ cup panko breadcrumbs
¾ cup parmesan, grated
1 tsp paprika

1 tsp garlic powder
1 egg, beaten
salt, to taste

1 Slice the zucchini into fries, leaving the skin on.

2 In a bowl, combine the breadcrumbs, parmesan, paprika, garlic powder and salt. Put the beaten egg in another bowl.

3 Coat the zucchini fries in the beaten egg, shaking off any excess, then roll them in the mixed crumb to coat evenly.

4 Air-fry at 400°F for 9 minutes – keep an eye on them to make sure they don't burn.

I have always loved popcorn chicken, but I recently had a version of it like this in Sardinia with a honey and lime dressing and, oh wow, does it make this even more delicious. Serve the dressing on the side for people to dip into and you've got a serious crowd-pleaser on your hands.

POPCORN CHICKEN
WITH A HONEY & LIME DRESSING

SERVES 4

½ tsp paprika
7 ½ cups rice puffs (like Rice Krispies) or cornflakes, blitzed or crushed into a fine crumb (you can also just use breadcrumbs)
2 eggs, beaten

4 chicken breasts, cut into small chunks
low-calorie oil spray
salt and pepper, to taste
Dressing
juice of 3 limes
5 tbsp honey

1 In a bowl, combine the paprika, crumb of choice and some seasoning. Put the beaten egg in another bowl.

2 Coat the chicken chunks in the egg, shaking off any excess, then roll them in the mixed crumb to coat evenly.

3 Spray well with low-calorie oil and air-fry at 400°F for 9 minutes.

4 Meanwhile, make the dressing by combining the lime juice and honey in a bowl, stirring well to mix.

5 Serve the popcorn chicken drizzled with the honey and lime dressing.

These are absolutely stunning and my twist on a dish that I order in a local restaurant. They taste sensational and, trust me, if you make these for visitors or for a party they will be one of the first things to be demolished. Salty feta with sweet honey really is the stuff of dreams.

HONEY FETA CUBES
WITH ROSEMARY

SERVES 4

2 eggs, beaten
1 ¼ cups all-purpose flour
1 ¾ cups panko or dried
   breadcrumbs, blitzed to
   a fine crumb
7 oz fat-reduced feta cheese,
   cut into cubes

6 tbsp honey
sprigs of rosemary, chopped,
   to sprinkle
sesame seeds, to sprinkle

1 Put the beaten egg, flour and breadcrumbs into three separate bowls. Coat the feta cubes first in the flour, then the egg, shaking off the excess, then roll them in the breadcrumbs to coat.

2 Air-fry at 375°F for 9 minutes.

3 Coat the cooked cubes in the honey – you can heat the honey first if you like.

4 Sprinkle with the chopped rosemary and sesame seeds. Pop a cocktail stick into each chunk and serve.

STARTERS & SNACKS

I wasn't sure whether to include this recipe in the book because these are so simple, but I actually have friends and family request these for parties. I find cooking sausages in the air fryer so effective – they come out perfectly and brown all over. I've used pork sausages here but you can use versions made with turkey or chicken if you want an even leaner starter.

HONEY MUSTARD COCKTAIL SAUSAGES

MAKES 40 SAUSAGES

40 cocktail sausages
low-calorie oil spray

4 tbsp honey
2 tbsp wholegrain mustard

1 Spray the sausages with a low-calorie oil. Cook them in the air fryer, evenly spread out – I usually preheat it for sausages – at 400°F for 12–14 minutes. If you are cooking sausages in large quantities, add more time.

2 Just before the last 2 minutes, combine the honey and mustard and pour over the sausages. (The air fryer basket will need to be cleaned after this, but it's worth it.)

STARTERS & SNACKS

I have made this recipe as chicken burgers with the breasts flattened and then as chicken tenders when I don't fancy a burger and want some dipping action – it's the same recipe, but cook the tenders for 12 minutes rather than 17 for the burger. For the tender recipe, there's no need to flatten the chicken breasts, just cut them into strips.

PARMESAN CHICKEN TENDERS

SERVES 4

3 chicken breasts, cut into strips
1 ¼ cups panko breadcrumbs
½ cup parmesan, grated
1 tsp paprika

1 tsp dried oregano
1 large egg, beaten
½ cup cornstarch
low-calorie oil spray
salt and pepper, to taste

1 Flatten the chicken breasts between two sheets of cling film with a rolling pin.

2 In a bowl, combine the breadcrumbs, parmesan, paprika, oregano and seasoning. Put the beaten egg in another bowl and the cornstarch in a third bowl.

3 Coat the chicken breasts in the flour, then the egg, shaking off any excess, then roll them in the breadcrumb mix.

4 Spray the crumbed chicken with the low-calorie oil and air-fry at 400°F for 15–17 minutes.

PER SERVING
99
CALORIES

I have to admit that I am a snacker (even when I'm snacking I'm thinking about my next snack)! This a great recipe to replace a bowl of nuts – gorgeous crunchy chickpeas that I can eat by the handful. If you can find it, wasabi powder is a great optional extra, as it adds real heat and I love the flavour.

CRUNCHY SPICED CHICKPEAS

SERVES 4

15-oz tin of chickpeas, drained
1 tsp paprika
pinch of salt
1 tsp oil or low-calorie oil spray

juice of ½ lemon
juice of ½ lime
1–2 tsp wasabi powder if you fancy a kick, you could use chilli powder (optional)

1 Blot the chickpeas with paper towels to remove any excess moisture. Transfer the chickpeas to a bowl and toss with all the other ingredients.

2 Air-fry at 400°F for 13–14 minutes. Check them for crispiness – you may need to cook them slightly longer depending on how crunchy you like them.

STARTERS & SNACKS

These dumplings are like little flavour bombs – amazing. They make a great starter if you're hosting a fakeaway night (see pages 120–149) but they are also incredible as a lunch or dinner. This recipe makes enough for a gathering, or you can batch cook and freeze these for yourself for a rainy day. They are gorgeous with rice, some greens and served with chilli oil and soy sauce.

CRISPY PORK DUMPLINGS
WITH CHILLI OIL

SERVES 6

1 lb lean ground pork
½ cup panko breadcrumbs
4 spring onions, sliced
3 tbsp soy sauce
1 tsp sesame oil
1 tsp garlic purée or 3 garlic
   cloves, crushed

1 tsp chilli flakes
½ tsp Chinese 5 spice
25–30 wonton papers
1 egg, beaten
low-calorie oil spray

1 In a bowl, combine the pork, breadcrumbs, spring onions, soy sauce, sesame oil, garlic, chilli flakes and 5 spice. (For extra flavour you can leave this to marinate in the fridge for a few hours or overnight.)

2 Lay the wonton papers flat and add the pork mix to the centre of each, trying not to fill them too much. You can fold over the papers in a samosa-style triangle or fold all the edges in at the top, don't be too precious about the shape. Rub the edges of the wonton papers with water and press firmly so the dumplings seal. Glaze them all over with the beaten egg.

3 Spray well with the low-calorie oil, ensuring you cover as much of the dumplings as possible.

4 Air-fry at 400°F for 10–12 minutes – closer to 12 minutes but check they don't burn. I turn mine halfway through and re-spray with the low-calorie oil.

This is the perfect alternative to a bag of crisps and dip, whether you're having a movie night in on your own or hosting friends – and it's much lower in calories, too. I sometimes substitute the oil for low-calorie oil spray which saves another 60 calories per portion.

PITTA CHIPS
WITH GUACAMOLE

SERVES 4

6 pitta breads (wholemeal
    also works)
2 tbsp oil
1 tsp paprika
grated mozzarella, for
    sprinkling (optional)
salt and pepper, to taste
Guacamole
1 onion, finely chopped
1 red chilli, chopped

2 avocados, mashed
handful of fresh coriander,
    chopped
5 garlic cloves, crushed
2 handfuls of cherry
    tomatoes, finely chopped
juice of 1 lime
juice of 1 lemon
1 tbsp oil
salt and pepper, to taste

1 Cut the pitta into triangles. In a bowl, mix the pittas with the oil, paprika and salt and pepper. Use your hands for this and just get in there to coat them all over.

2 Air-fry at 335°F for 12–14 minutes but shake halfway through, or if your air fryer doesn't have a drawer, just turn them.

3 While the pitta chips are cooking, combine all the guacamole ingredients in a bowl.

4 If you feel like it, sprinkle some mozzarella cheese into the air fryer basket during the last 2 minutes. Season with a little more salt and serve with the guacamole.

SPEEDY LUNCHES

This is such a quality work-from-home lunch. They are lovely with a salad or even in some wraps. Peanut sauce with coconut shrimp is a match made in heaven, but if you're not a fan of peanuts, you could also mix up some sweet chilli, honey, garlic and soy sauce for a honey chilli dressing.

COCONUT PANKO SHRIMP & PEANUT SAUCE

SERVES 4

1 cup panko breadcrumbs
2 tbsp desiccated coconut
½ cup flour
2 eggs, beaten
1 lb raw shrimp, peeled
low-calorie oil spray
salt and pepper, to taste

Peanut sauce
3 tbsp smooth peanut butter
⅔ cup water
juice of 1 lime
1 tbsp soy sauce
1 tsp garlic powder
1 tsp ground ginger

1 In a bowl, combine the breadcrumbs and coconut, and season with salt and pepper.

2 Put the flour into one bowl and the beaten egg in another. Coat the shrimp in the flour, then dip into the egg, shaking off any excess, then roll them in the breadcrumb mix to coat.

3 Spray really well with a low-calorie spray and air-fry at 400°F for 10 minutes.

4 While the shrimp are cooking, whip up your peanut sauce by combining all the ingredients in a bowl. Add some more water if it looks too thick.

5 Serve the shrimp with the peanut sauce.

PER SERVING
502
CALORIES

While this is a speedy lunch it also makes for an incredible breakfast or brunch. It's really versatile and you can make it more substantial by adding a poached egg or two and a slice of toasted sourdough.

SWEET POTATO & CHORIZO HASH

SERVES 3

1 ⅓ lb sweet potatoes, peeled and cut into cubes
1 tbsp oil or low-calorie oil spray
1 tbsp paprika
⅓ lb chorizo, sliced

1 tbsp light or half-fat butter
½ tsp chilli flakes
1 garlic clove, grated
4 tbsp Greek yogurt
salt and pepper, to taste
fresh dill, to sprinkle

1 In a bowl, combine the sweet potatoes, oil and paprika.

2 Air-fry the potatoes at 375°F for 14–15 minutes, and add the chorizo for the last 2–3 minutes.

3 While the chorizo is cooking, put the butter, chilli and garlic in a microwaveable bowl and microwave for 1 minute until the butter is melted.

4 Season the yogurt with salt and pepper.

5 Serve the hash drizzled with the yogurt, then top with the melted garlic chilli butter and sprinkle with fresh dill.

These are stunning and make lunchtime extra special, inspired by a version I had at a street food festival. They're so quick to make that they also work really well for dinner, especially if you're having friends round. They look so good that people will think you've spent ages cooking but the reality is, it's all done in 15 minutes.

HARISSA CHICKEN GYROS

SERVES 3

2 tbsp harissa paste
juice of 1 lemon
1 tsp paprika
1 tsp Cajun seasoning
1 tsp ground cumin
1 lb skinless, boneless chicken thighs
salt and pepper, to taste
3 supermarket gyros, flatbreads or pittas

handful of arugula
3 tbsp pomegranate seeds
small handful of pickled red onions (I use shop-bought – who has time to pickle stuff?)
Sauce
5 heaped tbsp Greek yogurt
juice of 1 lemon
2 garlic cloves, crushed

1 Combine the harissa, lemon juice, paprika, Cajun seasoning, cumin and salt and pepper in a bowl. Coat the chicken with this mixture – if you can, preheat the air fryer for 2–3 minutes because adding the chicken to the hot drawer will give it an extra bit of char. Air-fry at 400°F for 12 minutes.

2 While the chicken is cooking, combine the yogurt with the lemon juice and garlic.

3 Heat the gyros or flatbreads and assemble, stuffing with the chicken and arugula and drizzling over the yogurt sauce, then top with the pomegranate seeds and pickled red onions.

Caesar salad is one of my go-to meals, but it can be extremely calorific if you order one in a café – not to mention quite expensive – so here is a more cost-effective, leaner version. To make it even leaner, you could skip the parmesan and bacon and just have it with chicken, but either way it'll be ready in less than 15 minutes. Perfect all year round but even nicer on a sunny day.

CHICKEN CAESAR SALAD
WITH AIR-FRIED CROUTONS

SERVES 2

2 skinless, boneless chicken breasts
low-calorie oil spray
1 tsp dried oregano
1 tsp dried sage
4 strips of bacon
3 baby gem lettuce, leaves separated
1 cucumber, finely sliced
¼ cup parmesan shavings
salt and pepper, to taste

Croutons
½ tsp dried oregano
½ tsp paprika
2 slices of bread, cut into small squares

Dressing
4 tbsp light mayo
3 tbsp Greek yogurt
2 tbsp water
juice of 1 lemon
1 tsp dried oregano
1 tbsp Dijon mustard

1 Flatten the chicken breasts between two sheets of cling film with a rolling pin. Coat the chicken in the low-calorie spray, oregano and sage and season with salt and pepper. Cook in the air fryer at 400°F for 14 minutes.

2 Meanwhile, prepare the croutons. Add the oregano and paprika to a bowl and toss the bread squares in it to coat. For the last 8 minutes of the chicken cooking time, add in the bacon medallions, then 2 minutes later, add in the croutons.

3 Make the dressing by combining all the ingredients in a bowl.

4 Plate up the lettuce, cucumber, chicken and bacon, scatter over the parmesan and croutons and top with your dressing.

I know that all we use the air fryer in this recipe for is the bread, but this is so good, you need to try it. The speed of just throwing bread in the air fryer with some oil is why I love it. It's so simple, but one of the best lunches when I'm working from home.

TOMATO BRUSCHETTA

SERVES 4

4 slices of bread of choice (I always use a gorgeous ciabatta or olive loaf)
2–3 tbsp oil
2 good handfuls of cherry tomatoes, chopped
2 tbsp balsamic vinegar

handful of fresh basil leaves
2 tbsp grated parmesan, plus extra to serve
2 garlic cloves, 1 crushed and 1 cut in half
salt and pepper, to taste

1 Give the bread a drizzle of oil – about 2 tablespoons' worth – and use your hands to rub it all over the bread. Air-fry the bread at 375°F for 6 minutes.

2 Combine the rest of the ingredients in a bowl, except the cut garlic clove, for the topping.

3 When the bread is ready, rub the cut sides of the garlic halves along the crispy bread and top with the topping mixture.

4 Sprinkle with some more parmesan.

PER SERVING **555** CALORIES

While this isn't the most calorie-friendly recipe in the book, I'm all about balance. It's important to switch up leaner meals with those that are bit heartier otherwise you'll end up extra hungry and eating way over your calorie count by bingeing. This is one of my favourite sandwiches; I soften the onions in a pan beforehand but if you like them crunchy you can skip this step.

FRENCH ONION HAM & CHEESE SANDWICH

SERVES 2

1 tsp oil

1 tbsp light butter, plus extra for buttering

1 large white onion or 2 small or medium onions, sliced

small sprinkle of fresh thyme leaves

1 tsp Worcestershire sauce

4 slices of your chosen bread (I use a thick pan loaf or a sourdough)

2 slices of reduced-fat Cheddar

4 slices of Gruyère (grated works too)

4 slices of thin-sliced cooked ham

handful of grated reduced-fat mozzarella

salt and pepper, to taste

1 Heat the oil and butter in a pan and soften the onion with the thyme, Worcestershire sauce and some seasoning.

2 Butter the bread on both sides. Layer up each sandwich with the Cheddar and gruyère cheeses, ham and softened onions and press down firmly, I use the back of a chopping board to get it even, then top the bread with the mozzarella.

3 Cook in the air fryer at 375°F for 7 minutes.

EACH 258 CALORIES

These tasty guys were one of my go-to work-from-home lunches during lockdown, based on one of my favourite Spanish dishes, empanadas. I've swapped out the pastry for tortilla wraps for a calorie-cutting corner. Make as many as you like depending on how well you stuff them, I usually get 8 but you could get more or less based on the size of tortillas you use.

CHICKEN, CHORIZO & JALAPEÑO PARCELS

MAKES 8

1 ½ cup cooked chicken, shredded with forks or chopped into chunks

¼ lb cooked chorizo

3 tbsp tomato purée

3 tbsp sriracha

1 tsp paprika

3 jalapeños, sliced, (I used some from a jar)

1 red pepper, finely diced

1 cup mozzarella, grated (optional)

8 mini tortilla wraps (I've also used the larger ones plenty of times)

1 egg, beaten

salt and pepper, to taste

1 In a bowl, combine the chicken with all ingredients apart from the wraps and egg.

2 Add the filling to the middle of the wraps and fold over the sides and ends to make a parcel.

3 Brush with the beaten egg and press down the edges of the wrap with a fork tightly, we don't want any leaky parcels. Air-fry at 350°F for 9–10 minutes.

The mozzarella is optional, but it's a great addition if you want some cheesy action when you pull apart the parcels.

Salmon in the air fryer is your new best friend: crispy on the outside and flaky on the inside, and such a quick and easy lunch. Perfect for a busy day. I love salmon paired with orange, so I hope you enjoy this as much as I do.

HONEY & ORANGE SALMON

SERVES 2

2 salmon fillets
3 tbsp honey
2 tbsp orange juice

1 tbsp soy sauce
1 tsp crushed or grated garlic
1 orange, sliced

1 Pat dry the salmon fillets with some paper towels.

2 Combine the honey, orange juice, soy sauce and garlic in a bowl to make a sauce and pour it over the salmon as a glaze (it's runny, but that's ok).

3 Place the orange slices over the salmon and cook in the air fryer at 400°F for 12 minutes, reglazing the salmon with its glaze and juices halfway through for maximum flavour.

For extra crispy salmon, add a teaspoon of extra honey on top of the orange glaze.

This is one of those recipes I posted that went viral, but it's more of a hack than a recipe. If you're a fan of deep-dish pizza but are trying to keep an eye on calories, these are a must-make.

PEPPERONI PIZZA BAGELS

SERVES 2

2 bagels
2 tbsp tomato purée
1 tsp dried basil or oregano
1 oz pepperoni slices

small serving of light
    mozzarella (roughly ¾
    cup), grated
fresh basil leaves, to garnish

1 Cut the bagels in half and spread the bottom half of each with the tomato purée.

2 Top with the herbs, pepperoni slices and cheese – try to add the cheese last – it will keep the pepperoni in place as it melts because air fryers blow air in and the slices might fall off.

3 Air-fry at 350°F for 5–6 minutes and serve sprinkled with fresh basil.

While amazing in the air fryer, you can also cook these in the oven for 15 minutes at 350°F.

EACH **165** CALORIES

Made in five minutes, say hello to your new go-to lunch in a rush. I use soft taco shells for these and the rolls come out a bit like a taquito. There are no fancy or hard-to-find ingredients here and you can swap the chicken with veg or even tofu for a vegetarian version. Anything involving rolling wraps is good to get the kids to help with, so these are perfect for those weeks when they are off school.

BUFFALO CHICKEN & CHEESE ROLLS

MAKES 5

5 soft taco shells
1 ½ cup cooked chicken, shredded
Frank's RedHot sauce (get Buffalo if you can), for drizzling

⅔ cup grated reduced-fat mozzarella
low-calorie oil spray

1 Lay out the wraps and add the chicken, sauce and cheese into the middle of each, then roll or fold the sides tightly to create a rolled parcel.

2 Spray all over with low-calorie spray and air-fry at 400°F for 5 minutes.

While I do love a baked potato in the slow cooker, nothing beats the air-fryer to get that ultra-crispy outside and perfectly fluffy interior. There's no need to microwave the potatoes beforehand or preheat the fryer, you just pop them in. Couldn't be simpler.

AIR-FRIED BAKED POTATOES
WITH SALMON & SWEET CHILLI

SERVES 2

2 baking potatoes or russet
   potatoes
low-calorie oil spray
1 tsp garlic powder

To serve
light butter
½ lb cooked salmon, flaked
2 tbsp sweet chilli sauce
salt and pepper, to taste

1 Spray the potatoes with oil and sprinkle over some salt and garlic powder.

2 Air-fry at 400°F for 45 minutes, shaking them halfway through. For extra-large potatoes, cook them for 47 minutes.

3 Top with light butter, salt and pepper, add your flaked salmon and drizzle with the sweet chilli sauce.

I'm *obsessed* with these. A friend actually made these bagels for me and stuffed them with cheese and ham for lunch one day and I loved them, so I decided to take it further with new flavours.

BAGELS
WITH PERI-PERI CHICKEN & JALAPEÑOS

SERVES 4

1 cup self-raising flour,
   plus extra for dusting
1 cup Greek yogurt
1 egg
1 tbsp light butter
1 tbsp sesame seeds

Filling
3 cups cooked chicken, sliced
   or shredded
4 tbsp peri-peri sauce
   (bought is fine)
Cheddar slices (optional)
4 jalapeños, sliced (optional)

1 In a bowl, mix the flour, yogurt and egg – if it's too runny, add some extra flour until it resembles a dough you can roll.

2 Tip out onto a floured surface and knead for around 1 minute.

3 Divide into 4 portions, roll each into a sausage and shape into bagel rings.

4 Melt the butter in the microwave for 1 minute and brush it over the bagels to glaze, then scatter each with the seeds.

5 Air-fry at 375°F for 10 minutes – I can fit two bagels in each drawer so you may need to do this twice if your air fryer is smaller. They are ready when they have doubled in size and are gorgeously golden.

6 Slice in half once slightly cooled and fill with the chicken, sauce, cheese and jalapeños, if using, although I must confess these on their own with just ham and butter are incredible.

I love a frittata and here the time-consuming process of making it in the pan and finishing it in the oven is made much easier with the use of your air fryer. (If your air fryer is like mine and has a basket with a solid base, remove the grill at the bottom and just use the basket base.) The flavours of the classic Italian Caprese salad makes this a great summer lunch.

CAPRESE FRITTATA

SERVES 2

6 large eggs
2 handfuls of small
   mozzarella pearls
1 tsp dried oregano
15 cherry tomatoes, halved

1 onion, finely chopped
handful of fresh basil or basil
   oil
salt and pepper, to taste

1 Whisk the eggs together in a bowl or jug, then stir in the mozzarella and oregano and season to taste.

2 Air-fry the tomatoes and onion at 375°F for 5 minutes.

3 Pour in the eggs and mozzarella pearls and air-fry at 375°F for 25–30 minutes, however cover with foil for the first 22 minutes so the cheese doesn't burn.

4 Remove the frittata from the air fryer with a spatula.

5 Serve topped with fresh basil or some basil oil.

I love this recipe, and once again it is inspired by me trying to have more veggie days. The flavour combination of falafels with pickles, eggplant, tahini and the spices is honestly one of my favourites. It is absolutely gorgeous and everything can be cooked in the air fryer, right down to toasting the pittas.

FALAFELS IN PITTA
WITH TAHINI SAUCE & PICKLES

SERVES 5

2 x 15-oz tins of chickpeas, drained
handful of coriander, roughly chopped
1 tsp oil
1½ tsp ground cumin
1 onion, finely chopped
3 garlic cloves, crushed
½ tsp ground cinnamon
1 tsp paprika
juice of 1 lemon
3 tbsp flour
salt and pepper, to taste
low-calorie oil spray

Tahini sauce
6 tbsp plain yogurt
3 tbsp tahini
1 tsp chilli powder
3 tbsp light mayo
juice of 1 lime

Extras
1 eggplant, thinly sliced
½ tsp each paprika and ground cumin
5 pitta breads
¾ cup hummus
2 large tomatoes, thinly sliced
cornichons

1 Put all the falafel ingredients into a food processor and blitz to combine, then shape into roughly 20–25 balls. If your air fryer is small that's ok, just cook in two batches.

2 Spray the balls well with a low-calorie oil and air-fry at 350°F for 15 minutes.

3 Coat the eggplant slices in paprika and cumin, them drop them into the air fryer for the last 8–10 minutes of the falafel cooking time.

4 Add the pittas for the last 1 minute or just toast them separately.

5 Meanwhile, make the tahini sauce by combining all the ingredients.

6 Fill the pittas with the falafels, hummus, sliced tomato, pickles, eggplant slices and the tahini sauce.

These always take me back to my childhood, or even my university days. You can use cod in place of salmon here, just make sure that whichever fish you choose you get a thick fillet so you can cut it into fingers without it falling apart. Serve with tartare sauce or just ketchup or relish, or go one better and make yourself a fish finger sandwich.

SALMON FISH FINGERS

SERVES 4

1 lb skinless salmon fillets
2 tbsp flour
2 eggs, beaten

1 ¾ cups breadcrumbs mixed
    with 1 tsp ground turmeric
salt and pepper, to taste

1 Slice the salmon into fingers, then pat dry with paper towels.

2 Set the flour, egg and breadcrumbs into three separate bowls. Coat the salmon fingers with the flour, then dip into the beaten egg, shaking off the excess, then roll in the breadcrumbs to coat.

3 Air-fry at 400°F for 12 minutes, turning them halfway through.

This is inspired by a Japanese recipe I tried once and it's one of those veggie dishes that really delights. I've talked before about how I try to have a veggie day at least once a week, and this is a dish that crops up regularly. It's tasty, well-seasoned and has added sweetness from the honey and pomegranate.

HONEY, MISO & SOY EGGPLANT

SERVES 2

2 medium eggplants
2 tbsp honey
1 tsp miso
2 tbsp soy sauce
½ tsp ground cumin
1 tsp sesame oil

1 tsp sesame seeds
handful of pomegranate
   seeds (optional)
Sliced spring onions and
   coriander, to garnish

1 Cut the eggplants in half, then half again, then criss-cross the insides with a sharp knife – just lightly scoring them on the top, don't cut too deep. (This step is optional.)

2 Combine the honey, miso, soy, cumin and sesame oil in a bowl.

3 Glaze the eggplant with the sauce and air-fry at 350°F for 14–15 minutes, these will come out gorgeously brown and soft on the inside.

4 Sprinkle over the sesame seeds, spring onions, coriander and some pomegranate seeds, if you like, to add some sweetness.

I adore asparagus and this air-fried version makes for a perfect brunch when served on toast with a poached egg. If I'm really feeling those brunch vibes, I'll serve this with hollandaise sauce, but if you're being calorie conscious a good runny poached egg with a scattering of seeds will do. Another quick elevation of flavour is to give it a lashing of hot sauce.

LEMON PEPPER ASPARAGUS

SERVES 2

1 bunch of asparagus
zest and juice of 1 lemon
low-calorie oil spray

2 eggs (optional)
hollandaise sauce (optional)
salt and pepper, to taste

1 Chop the bottom chunky ends off the asparagus and coat in the lemon zest and juice. Sprinkle over the seasoning and spray with the oil. Air-fry at 400°F for 6–7 minutes.

2 While the asparagus fries, if you are serving with eggs, cook your poached eggs to your liking and serve with the hollandaise sauce.

These are absolutely divine and so easy to make – one of my all-time go-to lunches. Salmon is a low-calorie protein and perfect to fill you up, whether at lunch or dinner. I use supermarket bao buns, but if hard to find, these will easily work in some mini tortillas or even some steamed pancakes. Or you could skip that and pair it with a salad, as the salmon on its own really sings – it's sweet, sticky and just gorgeous.

TERIYAKI SALMON BAO BUNS

**MAKES 8 BAO BUNS –
SERVES 4**

2 large salmon fillets
2 tbsp teriyaki sauce
1 tbsp soy sauce
1 tbsp honey
8 bao buns
1 cucumber, julienned
1 ½ cups edamame beans
   (available in most
   supermarkets)

large handful of lettuce
   leaves
1 tbsp white sesame seeds
salt and pepper, to taste

Sauce
4 tbsp light mayo
3 tbsp sweet chilli sauce
1 tbsp soy sauce

1 Remove the skin from the salmon fillets and cut them into small chunks.

2 Combine the teriyaki sauce, soy sauce, honey and salt and pepper and add the salmon chunks, coating them all over. Air-fry at 375°F for 10 minutes.

3 While the salmon is cooking, combine all the sauce ingredients in a bowl and heat the bao buns following the packet instructions – supermarket bao buns can be microwaved or warmed in a steamer, if you have one.

4 Slice the buns and fill each with the salmon, veg and salad leaves, then drizzle with the dressing and sprinkle with the sesame seeds.

SPEEDY LUNCHES

Another easy and traditional tapas recipe, these garlic and chilli shrimp are sensational and so quick to make. This is a great sharing recipe, but I've definitely eaten this on my own. Ready in less than 15 minutes, it's perfect served with a bit of crusty bread.

PRAWN PIL PIL

SERVES 2

4–5 tbsp extra virgin olive oil
1 tsp paprika
1 tsp chilli flakes
3 garlic cloves, finely sliced
½ lb raw shrimp, peeled

a few slices of bread
(focaccia or crusty
sourdough is perfect)
handful of chopped parsley
salt and pepper, to taste

1 To an ovenproof dish, add the oil, paprika, chilli flakes, garlic, salt and pepper. Add this to the air fryer at 400°F for 8–10 minutes so the oil becomes super-hot, there's no need to preheat.

2 Carefully add the shrimp to the oil and stir in the oil with a spoon to coat – be very careful here as the oil will be hot. Cook for 5 minutes in the air fryer.

3 Toast your bread in the air fryer for 5 minutes, if required, and give everything a good sprinkle with the parsley. Serve with the bread to scoop up the shrimp and flavoured oil.

WEEKDAY
DINNERS

This takes inspiration from the flavours of jerk chicken, though the traditional dish is made with Scotch bonnet peppers. They can be hard to find in supermarkets, so this is my version, which works perfectly in an air fryer, although it can be baked in the oven too. Paired with gorgeous coconut rice, this really is something else.

SPICY CHICKEN DRUMSTICKS
WITH COCONUT RICE

SERVES 4

12 chicken drumsticks (or use wings, thighs or breasts)
1 tsp paprika
1 tsp chilli flakes
1 tbsp brown sugar
1 tsp dried parsley
1 tsp pumpkin pie spice
1 tsp ground cumin
1 tsp onion powder
1 tsp garlic powder
1 tsp ground ginger

2 tbsp oil, for cooking
juice of 1 lime
handful of fresh coriander, to garnish
Coconut rice
1 ½ cups rice
13.5-oz tin of reduced-fat coconut milk
15-oz tin of kidney beans, drained (optional)

Calories are based on chicken drumsticks and don't include the optional tin of kidney beans.

1 Combine all the ingredients for the chicken except the lime juice and oil, and coat the drumsticks in the mix. Cover and pop in the fridge for a few hours or overnight to marinate.

2 Drizzle the oil over the chicken and air-fry at 400°F for 22–25 minutes, turning halfway through.

3 Bring the rice to a boil in a pan of water and the coconut milk, then simmer over a low–medium heat for 15–20 minutes until cooked to your liking. Add the beans for the last few minutes to warm through, if using. Drain.

4 Pour the lime juice over the cooked chicken to give it some extra flavour. Serve the chicken and rice garnished with the coriander.

This is potentially one of the easiest recipes in the book, but it gives you flavour in spades. With minimal prep time, this goes perfectly with anything from salads to fries or potatoes. If I get home from work and find myself tempted to order a takeaway, this is one of my favourite speedy go-to meals. Serve with a side of your choice or some salad.

PEPPERONI & PESTO-STUFFED CHICKEN BREASTS

SERVES 2

2 skinless, boneless chicken breasts
1 tbsp Cajun seasoning
8 large slices of pepperoni

2 tsp red pesto
½ cup mozzarella cheese, grated
salt and pepper, to taste

1 Coat the outside of the chicken breasts in the Cajun seasoning, then cut down the side of each piece of chicken so you can stuff them. Fill the cavity with the pepperoni, pesto and mozzarella, then make sure the chicken breast is fully closed around the filling or the pepperoni will overcook.

2 Preheat the air fryer for 1 minute, then cook the chicken breasts at 375°F for 16–17 minutes.

These beetroot burgers never disappoint – even those who love a meaty burger will be satisfied. You can be creative and replace the beetroot with another veg of your choice if you prefer – try zucchini, cauliflower or whatever is in season. These are perfect for lunch or dinner on any day of the week. Serve with salad, sweet chilli sauce and some skinny fries.

BEETROOT BURGERS

SERVES 4

14.5 beetroot from a jar, drained

15-oz tin of chickpeas, drained

small handful of fresh coriander and mint

1 red onion, chopped

1 carrot, peeled and grated

2 garlic cloves, grated

1 large egg or 2 medium eggs

½ cup oats

1 tbsp oil

juice of ½ lemon

1 ⅓ cup crumbled feta

low-calorie oil spray

salt and pepper, to taste

glossy brioche buns, to serve

1 Dry the beetroot with paper towels – you don't want the patties too wet.

2 In a food processor, blitz all the burger ingredients except the feta, then crumble in the feta. Shape the mixture into 4 burgers.

3 Preheat the air fryer to 400°F, spray the burgers with low-calorie oil and cook for 10–12 minutes so they are nice and crispy, turning halfway if required.

4 Serve the burgers in brioche buns with your preferred side and accompaniments.

This is such a gorgeous dinner, perfect for any night of the week as it can be on the table in less than 15 minutes. This is a real childhood memory meal for me, as my nana made me minted lamb on a Sunday because I always requested it. These are absolutely gorgeous with baby boiled potatoes or cubed potatoes (see page 166) and some side salad or other veg.

LAMB CHOPS
WITH A MINT SAUCE

SERVES 4

2 tbsp oil
3 garlic cloves, grated
handful of chopped fresh
  mint
fresh rosemary, finely
  chopped

1 ½ lb lamb lamp chops,
  or a rack
  of lamb, cut into slices
salt and pepper, to taste

1 In a bowl, combine the oil, garlic, mint and rosemary and season with salt and pepper. Coat the lamb in the mixture.

2 Preheat the air fryer for 2–3 minutes so the chops get a sizzle when they first go in. Air-fry the lamb chops at 350°F for 10 minutes or to your preference. If you want them more charred then cook for 12 minutes, but you don't want them overcooked.

3 Let the lamb rest for 3 minutes before serving.

This will really jazz up your dinners during the week and trick anyone into thinking you just might have ordered in! Serve with noodles and sprinkle with sliced spring onions and red chilli. The beef is crispy and it's no surprise that sriracha and honey is a match made in heaven. You can also make this recipe with chicken tenderloins, cooking these for 15 minutes rather than the shorter duration for beef.

CRISPY SWEET CHILLI BEEF

SERVES 3

1 lb thin-cut beef steaks, cut into strips
2 tbsp cornstarch
low-calorie oil spray
1 onion, cut into chunks
handful of sugar snap peas or snow peas, halved lengthways

Sauce
3 tbsp sriracha
3 tbsp hoisin sauce
3 tbsp honey
4 garlic cloves, crushed
1 tsp rice wine vinegar
1 tbsp sesame oil
2 tbsp sweet chilli sauce

1 Dust the beef strips with the cornstarch, spray well with the low-calorie oil and air-fry at 375°F for 8–10 minutes – if you want it even crispier, keep it in for longer.

2 While the beef is cooking, soften the onion and greens over a medium heat in a pan sprayed with a low-calorie oil.

3 Once the beef is cooked, add this to the pan and pour in all the sauce ingredients. Cook over a medium heat for 1–2 minutes to heat through and let the sauce thicken.

Serving this with 1 cup of noodles will add 207 calories per serving.

PER SERVING
318
CALORIES

I'm pretty sure when you think of your childhood school-night dinners a chicken Kiev would definitely have made an appearance. I want to give you two options here: if you want the quickest version and don't mind the filling oozing slightly, use chicken breasts, otherwise, if you are precious about making sure not one drop of butter leaks out, use ground chicken. If you can't find ground chicken in the supermarket, ground turkey is a good alternative.

GARLIC CHICKEN KIEV

SERVES 4

4 tbsp light butter
6 garlic cloves, minced
handful of finely chopped
    fresh parsley
4 chicken breasts or 1 lb
    ground chicken with
    1 tsp cream cheese

1 egg, beaten
1 cup breadcrumbs
low-calorie oil spray
salt and pepper, to taste

Adding cream cheese to the ground chicken is a tip I found on a recipe forum – it adds moisture to the meat.

1 Make the garlic butter by mashing together the butter, garlic, parsley, salt and pepper in a bowl with a fork. Transfer the mixture to the middle of a strip of cling film and roll into a sausage shape. Place in the freezer for 2 hours or overnight to firm up.

2 Butterfly the chicken breasts, then open them up and place a slice of the butter in each and fold back over to cover. If using ground chicken, use your hands and form the chicken into a Kiev shape around the butter slice.

3 Place the egg and the breadcrumbs in two separate bowls. Dip the chicken Kiev into the beaten egg, shaking off any excess, then roll in the breadcrumbs to coat. Spray well with low-calorie spray and air-fry at 400°F for 22 minutes.

4 If your Kievs have oozed too much butter, remove the chicken and pour over the melted butter in the air-fryer tray (make sure your air fryer is clean, we don't want all sorts of crumbs on these work-of-art Kievs!).

I won't roast a chicken in the oven ever, ever again. This air-fryer version gives you a much crispier result and is so tender it just falls off the bone. It's perfect for any meal and any day, whether it's lunch or dinner, and the leftovers are great for meal prep. If you start by cooking the chicken breast-side down, the end result will be juicier.

ROTISSERIE-STYLE WHOLE CHICKEN

SERVES 4

1 tbsp olive oil
1 tsp paprika
1 tsp dried oregano

1 tsp dried basil
1 medium whole chicken
salt and pepper, to taste

1 Combine the oil, paprika, oregano, basil, salt and pepper in a bowl and glaze the whole chicken with it using a small brush.

2 Air-fry the chicken breast-side down at 375°F for 50 minutes – spray or grease the base of the air fryer to prevent the skin sticking, it may stick ever so slightly. You can also skip cooking it breast-side down and cook it upright for the whole duration, if you prefer.

3 Turn the chicken, and if you can baste it with the oil at the bottom of the drawer do so. Then roast for another 15 minutes (still at 375°F).

The timings given are for a medium chicken; if you are cooking a larger bird, you may need slightly longer. Always check whether a chicken is cooked by piercing the thigh with the tip of a sharp knife – if the juice runs clear it is cooked; if not, cook it a little longer.

These are so refreshing, light and perfect for a summer dinner. So easy to make – cooking doesn't get much simpler than this. I made this for two but it could stretch to three portions. It's great served with flatbread, sliced tomatoes, fresh basil leaves and a dollop of tzatziki.

LEMON GARLIC CHICKEN KEBABS

SERVES 3

1 tbsp garlic powder
juice of 2 lemons
1 tsp dried oregano
1 tsp fresh or dried rosemary

3 tbsp plain yogurt
2 tbsp oil
1 lb boneless chicken thighs
salt and pepper, to taste

1 Combine the garlic powder, lemon juice, oregano, rosemary, yogurt, oil and salt and pepper. Coat the chicken in the mixture, then leave to marinate in the fridge for a few hours if you can, but if you can't wait, don't worry.

2 Cook in the air fryer at 400°F for 20 minutes.

The calories have been calculated to include the flatbread, tzatziki and tomato serving suggestions (as pictured).

Crispy and full of flavour, this is a great one for family and friends and, thanks to the quicker cook time of an air fryer, you can make it any day of the week. You can keep it as one whole joint or cut it into smaller pieces to reduce the cooking time. The Chinese 5 spice gives it that gorgeous aromatic flavour and the salt and sugar gives the skin that sweet and salty crunch.

CRISPY & AROMATIC PORK BELLY

SERVES 5

2 ¼ lb pork belly, skin on
1 tbsp Chinese 5 spice
1 tsp garlic powder

2 tbsp honey
1 tbsp sea salt flakes

1 Pat the pork dry with some paper towels – this step is super important as it helps the pork get extra crispy.

2 Pierce tiny holes in the skin using a skewer or fork, being careful not to go through to the flesh.

3 Rub the Chinese 5 spice over the pork flesh and the garlic powder, honey and salt across the skin.

4 Wrap the pork completely in foil and air-fry at 400°F for 1 hour 5 minutes.

5 Remove the foil and air-fry for another 10–12 minutes, if required, to crisp up that gorgeous skin.

6 Serve with a salad or your side of choice or even some homemade fries.

Any leftovers can be used in a variety of meals like bao buns, pittas, with salad or with steamed green veg.

While I make this with chicken, it can also be made with beef or pork – in fact, pork might be the most popular choice out there. You can serve this with rice or noodles as a delicious and easy midweek meal. You might even think you have ordered in a takeaway, it's just that good!

KUNG PAO CHICKEN

SERVES 4

3 skinless chicken breasts, cut into chunks
1–2 tbsp soy sauce
3–4 tbsp cornstarch
½ tsp Chinese 5 spice
low-calorie oil spray
1 onion, cut into chunks
1 red pepper, chopped
1 green pepper, chopped
1 carrot, cut into strips
chopped spring onions and peanuts, to garnish

Sauce
4 tbsp soy sauce
1 tbsp Shaoxing wine
1 tsp ginger purée
1 tbsp hoisin sauce
1 tbsp sriracha
1 tsp chilli flakes
½ cup water
1 tbsp cornstarch
2 tbsp honey
3 garlic cloves, crushed

Serving with 1 ¼ cups of rice will increase the calories per serving by 260 calories.

1 Put the chicken in a lidded container with the soy sauce, cornstarch and Chinese 5 spice, pop the lid on and shake to coat.

2 Spray the chicken really really well with low-calorie oil and air-fry at 400°F for 12–14 minutes, shaking halfway to stop it sticking.

3 When the chicken is almost ready, start to soften the veg in a pan over a low heat.

4 Once the chicken is cooked, add it to the pan and pour in all the sauce ingredients. Garnish with the spring onions and peanuts.

I absolutely love tacos, and given my choice of filling, I'll always go with cod. These are simply gorgeous and feel so fresh with the zesty lemon and lime flavours. You can really play around with this recipe – change the protein, add mango or chilli, make them totally veggie – the possibilities are endless.

FISH TACOS

MAKES 8 TACOS

Fish
1 ½ lb cod fillets
1 ¼ cup water
1 egg
1 ½ cups all-purpose flour
1 tsp baking powder
1 tsp lemon pepper
  seasoning or lemon zest
salt and pepper, to taste

Sauce
6 tbsp light mayo
3 tbsp Greek yogurt
2 tbsp sriracha
juice of 1 lime
1 tsp paprika
1 tsp garlic powder

To serve
soft or hard-shell tacos
lettuce
tomatoes
red onion
coriander
guacamole (see page 46)

1 Season the cod fillets with salt and pepper.

2 In a bowl, beat the water, egg, flour, baking powder and seasoning or zest.

3 Coat the fish in the batter, then cook in a preheated air fryer at 400°F for 14–16 minutes – it's important that the air fryer is piping hot as the fish goes in. Check after 10 minutes to ensure nothing burns – mine usually take 15 minutes.

4 While the fish is frying, combine all the sauce ingredients in a bowl and prep your filling ingredients.

5 Assemble the tacos with the fish, veg and guacamole and top with the sauce.

The first time I tried a mango and jalapeño sauce was actually with chicken wings, but I liked it so much I now use it with so many meals. Halloumi works really well with any sauce or dressing that is sweet and sticky, so it's a perfect combination here. Pair these with some fresh crunchy veg, sour cream and coriander.

HALLOUMI FAJITAS
WITH A MANGO & JALAPEÑO SAUCE

MAKES 6 FAJITAS

1 tbsp oil
1 tsp ground cumin
1 tbsp paprika
1 tsp chilli powder
1 tsp dried oregano
8.8 oz block of halloumi, cut into thin chunks
1 red pepper, cut into thin chunks
1 yellow pepper, cut into thin chunks
1 onion, cut into chunks
6–8 tortillas (I prefer soft taco shells)

fresh coriander, to garnish
6 tsp sour cream (optional)
salt and pepper, to taste

Sauce

1 mango, peeled and chopped
2 tbsp mango chutney
1–2 jalapeños, add more if you like
1 white onion, roughly chopped
5 tbsp water (or more, to loosen it up)
2 garlic cloves

If you prefer, mix together some mango chutney, sweet chilli sauce and jalapeño paste as a shortcut, but the homemade paste is gorgeous.

1 In a bowl, combine the oil, cumin, paprika, chilli, oregano, salt and pepper. Coat the halloumi, peppers and onions with the seasoned oil.

2 Air-fry at 400°F for 8–10 minutes with the halloumi on the top of the peppers, if you can, so the peppers have a light char.

3 While the air fryer is on, blitz the ingredients for the mango and jalapeño sauce in a food processor to a chunky sauce.

4 Add the mix to your wraps, top with fresh coriander, the mango dressing and some sour cream if you like.

This is such a crowd-pleasing and comforting dish and it's super quick, too, which makes it perfect for a weekday dinner. Even better, it's so easy to make. Cook it for guests and they'll be so impressed. Garnish with fresh basil leaves and enjoy with your side of choice – salad, potatoes or even some pasta.

CHICKEN PARM
WITH A MARINARA SAUCE

SERVES 4

4 medium-sized skinless, boneless chicken breasts
½ cup cornstarch
2 large eggs, beaten
2 cups panko breadcrumbs
¾ cup parmesan, grated
low-calorie oil spray
¾ cup mozzarella cheese, grated

Marinara sauce
4 garlic cloves, crushed
14 oz marinara sauce
1 tbsp olive oil
1 tsp onion powder
1 tsp dried oregano
1 tsp dried rosemary
1 tbsp balsamic vinegar
salt and pepper, to taste

Serving with a ¾ cup portion of cooked spaghetti will add another 281 calories per person.

1 Flatten the chicken breasts between two sheets of cling film with a rolling pin.

2 Put the cornstarch, egg and breadcrumbs mixed with the parmesan in three separate bowls.

3 Dunk the chicken into the flour, then into the beaten egg, shaking off any excess, then roll in the breadcrumbs and parmesan mix to coat.

4 Spray well with the low-calorie oil, line the air-fryer with baking parchment, and cook at 400°F for 14 minutes.

5 While the chicken is cooking, soften the garlic in the oil in a saucepan before adding the remaining sauce ingredients.

6 Once the chicken is cooked, spoon over the sauce, top with the mozzarella and air-fry for 2 minutes to melt the cheese.

PER SERVING
323
CALORIES

It may seem weird to have a Sunday roast in the weekday dinners chapter, but thanks to the magic of the air fryer, this gorgeous roast beef can be ready in just over an hour – making midweek roasts totally possible. It's also great if you have been out on a Saturday night and just haven't had time to prep on Sunday morning. I recommend serving with mash, roasted cauliflower, carrots and some greens.

'FORGOT TO PREP' SUNDAY ROAST

SERVES 6

2 ¼ lb rump roast
1 tbsp oil
salt and pepper, to taste

1 Massage the beef with the oil and season well with salt and pepper. Preheat the air fryer to 400°F.

2 For the first 5 minutes, air-fry at 400°F to really help the outside crisp up, then lower the temperature to 350°F or the roast setting on your air fryer for 40 minutes.

3 Once the 40 minutes is up, lower the temperature to 285°F for 20 minutes.

4 I like roast beef slightly pink on the inside, but check your joint is cooked to your liking. You can keep the roast in for longer if you prefer it more well done.

Provided your air fryer is clean, use the juices at the bottom of the tray for your gravy. I also cook my roasties in the air fryer (see page 163).

This is such a great midweek meal and immediately reminds me of when I was younger, as it's something my mum used to make for me. I absolutely love this dish and it is so much faster in the air fryer than in the oven. This is gorgeous with some salad, couscous and corn on the cob.

PEPPERED PORK CHOPS

SERVES 4

4 pork chops
1–2 tbsp oil or a few squirts of a low-calorie oil spray
1 tsp steak seasoning
1 tbsp paprika
1 tsp onion powder
1 tsp dried parsley
1 tsp garlic powder
1 tsp crushed peppercorns
salt, to taste

1 Pat the chops dry with some paper towels, then coat them in the oil and all the seasonings.

2 Cook in an air fryer preheated to 400°F for 11–12 minutes. If the chops are extra large, cook for 14 minutes.

FAKEAWAYS

I know these are usually ordered as a side but sometimes I make them as a snack, starter or just to feed a craving. They are so good and this air-fryer version always hits the spot without the heavy calories you get from the more traditional takeaway variety.

ONION BHAJIS

MAKES 12

3 white onions, sliced
½ cup cornstarch
1 tbsp ground turmeric
1 tsp ground cumin
½ tsp ground coriander
1 tsp garam masala

1 tsp garlic purée or paste
½ thumb-sized piece fresh
   ginger, chopped
1 egg, beaten
salt and pepper, to taste

1 Wrap the onion slices in paper towels and pat dry to remove any excess moisture.

2 Combine all the ingredients in a bowl and mould with your hands into your desired shape to make 12 balls or patties. You may need to add a bit of additional water to help the mixture stick into balls.

3 Air-fry at 350°F for 15 minutes or until they've reached your desired level of crispiness. Feel free to cook them a tad longer if you prefer.

Nothing beats these, particularly when served with sweet chilli sauce for some dipping action. If I'm with a crowd of people and there is only one left, I will make every possible effort to politely take the last one. This air-fried, lower-calorie version completely justifies making these during the week, just because! If I am using fresh shrimp here and don't need them all I freeze the rest in sandwich bags.

JUMBO SHRIMP SESAME TOAST

SERVES 4

⅓ lb king shrimp, peeled and deveined
1 tsp garlic purée
1 tsp sesame oil
4 slices of white bread

1 tbsp white and black sesame seeds
2 eggs
low-calorie oil spray
fresh coriander, to garnish

1 If you have a food processor, blitz the shrimp, garlic and sesame oil to a paste. If you don't have one, chop up the shrimp with a sharp knife, then add to a bowl with the garlic and sesame oil and use a fork to squish the mix to a paste-like spread.

2 Spread the prawn paste over the bread, then dip the bread prawn-side down into the sesame seeds on a plate. Slice the bread into 4 smaller triangles.

3 In a wide bowl that you can fit the bread slices into, beat the eggs, then dip in the bread (not the prawn side) very briefly, gently shaking off any excess. You can skip this step if you like, I find it helps get the bread extra golden and crispy.

4 Add to the air fryer, prawn-side facing up, spray with low-calorie oil and cook at 400°F for 8 minutes.

5 Serve garnished with some fresh coriander.

I absolutely adore anything cooked in black bean sauce, and even though I love it most with beef, I've added chicken here as it's a bit leaner and less expensive. Crispy breaded chicken in a gorgeous, velvety black bean sauce is a meal I would happily eat every week without any complaints, served up with rice and a sprinkling of chopped spring onions.

CRISPY CHICKEN & BLACK BEAN SAUCE

SERVES 4

2 heaped tbsp cornstarch

1 egg, beaten

1 ¾ cups breadcrumbs (you can use panko breadcrumbs or even finely crushed cornflakes)

1 lb skinless chicken breasts, cut into thin strips

low-calorie oil spray

Veg

2.5oz mushrooms, quartered

1 green pepper, cut into chunks

1 onion, cut into chunks

15-oz tin of black beans, drained

Sauce

4 tbsp soy sauce

1 tsp oyster sauce

1 tbsp hoisin sauce

4 garlic cloves, crushed

1 ¼ cup chicken stock

½ thumb-sized piece ginger, freshly grated

1 tbsp cornstarch (optional – for a thicker sauce)

1 Put the cornstarch, egg and breadcrumbs into three separate bowls. Coat the chicken strips first in the cornstarch, then in the egg, shaking off any excess, then roll them in the breadcrumbs to coat.

2 Spray well with the low-calorie oil and air-fry at 400°F for 10–12 minutes – but check on them, as depending on how thin you cut the strips they could be ready earlier.

3 While the chicken is cooking, soften the chopped veg in a non-stick pan over a medium heat, then add in all the sauce ingredients and drained black beans and let this simmer until

heated through and slightly thickened.

4 Toss in the cooked chicken, stir into the sauce and heat through for a few minutes.

You could make this process a little quicker by shaking all the chicken pieces and cornstarch together in a lidded box, then coat them in the egg and breadcrumbs individually.

This is a BLT burger made with chicken coated in cornflakes (I'll let you decide if the C stands for cornflakes or chicken), which might sound strange but, oh my, it tastes absolutely incredible. This recipe makes two burgers but if I am home alone you can bet that I'll double up and eat both chicken breasts in one burger! The calories here include all the optional toppings. Feel free to leave them off for a slightly lighter version.

THE AIR FRYER CBLT BURGER

SERVES 2

2 eggs, beaten
3 cups cornflakes, crushed
1 tsp Cajun seasoning
1 tsp paprika
1 tsp dried oregano
1 tsp lemon salt (optional – it's tricky to get)
2 skinless, boneless chicken breasts

2 slices of bacon (feel free to add more)
2 brioche buns
slices of lettuce and tomato, light mayo, to serve
2 tsp green pesto (optional), to serve

You could make this process a little quicker by shaking all the chicken pieces and flour together in a lidded box, then coat them in the egg

1 Put the egg into one bowl. Put the cornflakes into another bowl and mix with the Cajun seasoning, paprika, oregano and lemon salt, if using.

2 Flatten the chicken breasts between two sheets of cling film with a rolling pin. Dip the chicken breasts into the egg, shaking off any excess, then roll in the seasoned cornflakes to fully coat.

3 Cook the chicken in the air fryer at 335°F for 17 minutes – don't have the temperature too high or you will burn the cornflakes (I check mine after 15 minutes and lower the temperature if required).

4 For the last 8–10 minutes of the chicken cooking time, add the bacon. My air fryer has two baskets so I do it in a separate drawer at 400°F. If you have one basket, cook the bacon at 335°F for 10–12 minutes – so add it 5 minutes after your burger.

5 Assemble the chicken into your brioche buns with the cooked bacon, lettuce, tomato and a dollop of mayo, adding some pesto if you like.

Most of us have had *that* katsu curry at *that* popular restaurant chain, but here is my version which you can make at home. This is perfect for during the week or even at the weekend so you don't need to order in – and it will save you some money. I love this with sweet potato but you can also make it with chicken (see note). Serve with basmati rice and a salad.

SWEET POTATO KATSU CURRY

SERVES 4

If you prefer not to blitz the sauce, just don't add a carrot to it.

If you are making this with chicken, use 4 chicken breasts and flatten them first, then air-fry for 14–15 minutes.

2 tbsp flour
2 eggs, beaten
1 cup panko breadcrumbs
1 ⅓ lb sweet potato, peeled and cut into long slices (in the shape of the potatoes)

Sauce
low-calorie oil spray
1 onion, roughly chopped
1 carrot, roughly chopped
1 tsp garlic powder

¾ cup chicken stock
13.5-oz tin of reduced-fat coconut milk
small chunk of fresh ginger, grated
2 tbsp soy sauce
2 tbsp curry powder
1 tsp ground turmeric
1 tsp granulated sweetener
1 tbsp cornstarch, if required
salt and pepper, to taste

1 First make the sauce. Spray the pan with a low-calorie oil and soften the onion and carrot in a pan over a medium heat, then add the remaining ingredients and let this simmer for 15 minutes. Blitz the sauce with a handheld blender until smooth.

2 Put the flour, egg and breadcrumbs into three separate bowls. Coat the potatoes in the flour, then in the beaten egg, shaking off any excess, then roll in the panko breadcrumbs.

3 Spray with low-calorie oil spray and air-fry at 375°F for 12 minutes.

4 Serve the cooked potatoes with the hot curry sauce.

PER SERVING
331
CALORIES

Sticky, sweet and a whole lotta goodness. This is my go-to when I fancy a Chinese takeaway but don't want to spend the money or want a less-calorific version. And it's ready in less than half an hour which is quicker than it would take to order in!

LEMON CHICKEN

SERVES 3

2 heaped tbsp cornstarch
1 tsp garlic powder
1 tsp ground ginger
3 skinless, boneless chicken
  breasts
low-calorie oil spray or 1 tbsp
  oil
Sauce
juice of 1 large lemon
3 tbsp honey

½ cup chicken stock
3 tbsp soy sauce
3 garlic cloves, crushed
1 tsp ground ginger
Garnish
spring onions
lemon slices
sesame seeds
sweet chilli crispy onions

1 Combine the cornstarch, garlic and ginger powders in a bowl and toss the chicken in this mix. Add to an air fryer with about 20 sprays of oil or 1 tablespoon of oil. Cook at 400°F for 20 minutes.

2 For the sauce, add all the ingredients to a pan and cook over a high heat until it starts to thicken. Coat the chicken in the sauce in the pan before serving. Add any or all of the garnishes listed above.

Serving with 1 ¼ cup of rice per person will add 260 calories to each serving.

I love Bang Bang Chicken more than I can say, and this is my at-home, air-fryer version. This makes for a versatile dinner, as you could add the chicken and sauce to a salad, pile it into a sandwich, or serve with noodles or rice. If you are in a rush, you can even just make the sauce and pair with some cooked, shredded chicken and add to a sandwich with cucumber and lettuce.

SPICY PEANUT CHICKEN

SERVES 3

½ cup cornstarch
1 tsp paprika
2 eggs, beaten
1 cup fresh or panko
   breadcrumbs
3 skinless chicken breasts,
   cut into small chunks
salt and pepper, to taste

Sauce
4 tbsp light mayo
1 tbsp soy sauce
1 tbsp honey
3 tbsp sweet chilli sauce
2 tbsp hot sauce
1 tbsp peanut butter
3 garlic cloves, crushed

1 Put the cornstarch and paprika, the egg and breadcrumbs into three separate bowls. Coat the chicken in the seasoned cornstarch, then in the egg, shaking off any excess, then roll in the breadcrumbs to coat. Cook in the air fryer at 400°F for 20–22 minutes.

2 While the chicken is cooking, combine all the sauce ingredients in a saucepan over a medium heat, stirring, until warmed through.

3 Serve the spicy chicken with the warm sauce.

I use high-fibre brown rolls for the breadcrumbs – I put two in my food processor and blitz them. They provide 120 calories each.

This is an amazing fakeaway – with all the crispiness you get from the deep-fat fried version and a good chilli and garlic flavour, but calorie friendly. While this recipe is amazing with beef it is also gorgeous with chicken; use the same weight of chicken, but note that it will take longer to cook than the beef – around 14–15 minutes. I can honestly say if honey chilli chicken or beef is on a menu I will definitely order it.

HONEY CHILLI BEEF

SERVES 3

1 lb thin-cut lean beef steaks, cut into strips
1 tbsp soy sauce
3 tbsp cornstarch with 1 tsp garlic granules and 1 tsp ground ginger
low-calorie oil spray
1 onion, cut into large chunks
1 red pepper, cut into large chunks
3 ½ cups rice, cooked

Sauce
5 tbsp orange juice
5 garlic cloves, crushed
5 tbsp honey
1 tsp chilli flakes
1 tbsp soy sauce
4 tbsp light soy sauce
1 tsp rice vinegar

Serving the beef with 1 ¼ cups of rice will add another 260 calories per person.

1 Coat the beef strips in the soy sauce then in the cornstarch, garlic and ginger mix. Spray really well with the low-calorie oil and air-fry at 400°F for 10 minutes.

2 While the beef is cooking, combine all the sauce ingredients in a bowl.

3 Once the beef is cooked, add the onion and pepper to a saucepan over a medium heat and cook for 5 minutes until softened, then add the sauce and stir in the beef.

4 Let the sauce thicken and coat the beef for a minute or two before serving with the rice.

This is such a beaut fakeaway that really hits the spot. It feels and tastes like a takeaway but the nutritional values say differently. If you want more of a sauce with this, you could always buy a jar of supermarket curry sauce and heat it through before adding to the chicken.

SALTED CHILLI CHICKEN

SERVES 2

1 egg, beaten
3 skinless chicken breasts, sliced lengthways
3 heaped tbsp cornstarch
1 tsp mild chilli powder
½ tsp Chinese 5 spice
1 tsp garlic powder
1 tbsp salt

1 tsp pepper
low-calorie oil spray
1 red pepper, cut into strips
1 onion, chopped
5 garlic cloves, crushed
1 tbsp soy sauce
1 tsp rice wine
1 tsp chilli flakes

1 Add the egg to a bowl and coat the chicken strips in the egg, shaking off any excess. In another bowl, combine the cornstarch, chilli powder, Chinese 5 spice, garlic powder, salt and pepper. Spray with the low-calorie oil and air-fry the chicken at 350°F for 15 minutes.

2 Once the chicken is cooked, fry the pepper and onion in a pan over a medium heat, then add the crushed garlic, soy sauce, rice wine and chilli flakes.

3 Add the chicken to the pan and stir to combine, cooking until everything is heated through.

Serving this with 1 ¼ cups of rice will add 260 calories per portion.

I am obsessed with doner kebabs, and like many people, these take me right back to university when I'd more than likely come home with one after a night out. It's such a classic takeaway which brings me so much happiness, so here is my fakeaway version. Serve with pitta or flatbread, and some lettuce, tomato and red onion slices. My chosen sauces are always a low-calorie garlic mayo and a chilli kebab sauce, or for convenience just a store-cupboard sriracha.

DONER KEBAB

SERVES 4

1 ¼ lb ground lamb
   (the leaner the better)
1 tsp ground cumin
1 tsp paprika
1 tsp chilli powder

1 tsp onion powder
1 tsp ground coriander
½ tsp dried oregano
3 garlic cloves, crushed

1 Combine the lamb in a bowl with all the spices and garlic and roll the mixture into a sausage shape.

2 Cook in the air fryer at 350°F for 35 minutes.

To make your own garlic mayo, just mix up some light mayo with some crushed garlic.

Calories have been calculated to include flatbreads and other suggested fillings.

468 CALORIES PER SERVING

Some people aren't a fan of sweet and sour (I don't get it!) but even if you aren't I reckon you'll love this dish. Juicy chicken in a super tasty sauce, what's not to love? I like to serve this with rice or noodles. Adding 1 cup rice will increase the calorie count to 624 calories per serving.

SWEET & SOUR CHICKEN

SERVES 3

1 egg, beaten
3 tbsp cornstarch
1 tbsp garlic powder
3 skinless chicken breasts, cut into chunks
1 onion, chopped
1 red pepper, cut into chunks
1 yellow pepper, cut into chunks
8-oz tin of water chestnuts, drained

Sweet and sour sauce
1 ¼ cup pineapple juice
½ cup water
⅓ cup rice wine vinegar
5 tbsp tomato ketchup (I used reduced sugar)
1 tbsp tomato purée
1 tbsp soy sauce
2 tbsp light soy sauce
1½ tbsp cornstarch
2–3 tbsp honey
3 garlic cloves, crushed

As a shortcut you could just add the sauce to some cooked low-calorie tenders or nuggets.

1 Put the egg in a bowl and combine the cornstarch and garlic powder in another bowl. Coat the chicken in the egg, shaking off any excess, then roll in the cornstarch mix to coat. Air-fry at 400°F for 12–15 minutes, depending on how small you've cut it.

2 While the chicken is cooking, combine all the sauce ingredients in a bowl.

3 Once the chicken is cooked, add the onion, peppers and water chestnuts to a pan over a medium heat to soften, then add the chicken and sauce and heat through. The sauce will thicken almost instantly and be ready to serve.

This is inspired by one of the most famous burgers in the world – you know the one. It's a filling version of one of your fast-food must-haves. It is definitely one for when you want to treat yourself, but you can use leaner beef patties for a slightly lower-calorie version.

'NOT A FAST FOOD BURGER'

SERVES 3

6 beef patties (use as lean as you want)
3 seeded buns, sliced in half
lettuce, red onion slices, pickled gherkin slices, Cheddar slices, to serve (optional)

Sauce (enough for 4 burgers)

4 tbsp mayo
3 tbsp ketchup
1 tsp garlic powder
1 tsp onion powder
1 tbsp Dijon mustard
1 tbsp pickle juice

1 This is so simple I'm not even sure I can call it a recipe! Anyhow, air-fry your burgers at 375°F for 12–15 minutes – 12 minutes for skinny burgers and 15 for those thicker bad boys.

2 While the burgers are cooking, mix up your burger sauce, which, might I add, is sensational.

3 Plate up the cooked patties into the seeded buns, 2 per bun, and add your preferred toppings and a dollop of sauce.

I think the first time I ever tried firecracker chicken was in Wagamama and I was blown away, I just knew I had to make my own version. This is perfect with noodles, rice or even just on its own with some veg if you are trying to cut down on carbs. I love it, and the addition of the sugar snap peas gives it some crunch. Serving with 1 ¼ cups of of rice (see note) would add 260 cals and a small handful of peanuts would add another 124 cals.

FIRECRACKER CHICKEN

SERVES 3

1 egg, beaten
3 heaped tbsp cornstarch
1 tsp garlic powder
¾ lb skinless chicken breasts, cut into chunks
low-calorie oil spray
⅓ lb sugar snap peas
salt and pepper, to taste

Sauce
4 garlic cloves, crushed
5 tbsp honey
6–7 tbsp sriracha
3 tbsp soy sauce
1 tbsp malt vinegar
1 tsp tamarind paste

This is great served with rice, spring onions, a lime wedge and some peanuts. I squeeze the lime over the bowls to help balance the heat.

1 Put the egg in a bowl and combine the cornstarch, garlic and seasoning in another bowl. Dip the chicken in the egg, then in the cornstarch and seasoning mix.

2 Fully coat the chicken in the low-calorie oil spray and air-fry at 400°F for 12–14 minutes – you want it really crispy.

3 While the chicken cooks, combine all the ingredients for the sauce in a bowl.

4 Around 1–2 minutes before the chicken is cooked, spray a wok or deep pan with the low-calorie oil and soften the sugar snap peas.

5 Add the chicken and the sauce to the peas and heat through until piping hot.

Who doesn't love duck pancakes? I'm obsessed with this recipe – it's so easy and requires hardly any skill or prep to make it. During lockdown I made my own pancakes, but these days I buy them from the supermarket. I normally cook poultry breast-side down, as it keeps the meat juicy, but for this dish you actually want it to dry out a bit so it becomes crispy.

WHOLE HOISIN DUCK
WITH PANCAKES

SERVES 4

1 whole duck
2 tbsp Chinese 5 spice
1 tsp oil
1 lime, cut in half
10 Chinese-style pancakes (can be found at Chinese supermarkets)

hoisin sauce, for dipping
spring onions, sliced into matchsticks
cucumber, sliced into matchsticks
salt and pepper, to taste

1 Coat the duck in the Chinese 5 spice and oil, and season with salt and pepper, pop the lime in the cavity and air-fry at 375°F for 55–60 minutes.

2 Let the duck rest at room temperature for 10 minutes – it will continue to slightly cook and dry out further.

3 Shred the duck with two forks and serve with the pancakes, hoisin sauce and veg.

If you're making this for two people or you're in a rush, you could use duck breasts instead of a whole duck, in which case follow the same process but cook in the air fryer for 35 minutes.

SIDES

I absolutely love corn on the cob, especially with butter, but pair it with a chimichurri dressing and it is exceptional. I know this is in the sides chapter, but it definitely isn't just as a side – you can have this on its own or as a gorgeous lunch paired with a salad.

CHIMICHURRI CORN ON THE COB

SERVES 4

4 corn on the cob
low-calorie oil spray
1 tbsp light or half-fat butter
Chimichurri dressing
handful of fresh parsley, chopped (the traditional option, but if I have basil I use that too)

3 tbsp olive oil
5 garlic cloves, crushed
1 red chilli, chopped
handful of cherry tomatoes, finely chopped
salt and pepper, to taste

1 Spray the corn with the low-calorie oil and spread it with the butter. Wrap the cobs in foil and air-fry at 350°F for 18-20 minutes.

2 Mix up the dressing ingredients and pour over the cooked corn.

If you would like the corn more charred, don't wrap them in foil, just add the melted butter once cooked.

This looks simple but it packs a real flavour punch. It's inspired by a dish I tried at an incredible Japanese restaurant I go to in Belfast where everyone always says 'try the broccoli!'. So here we are, my own homemade air-fryer version. I like to serve this with garlic aioli, which of course isn't Japanese but garlic just makes everyone happy!

TEMPURA BROCCOLINI

SERVES 4

½ cup all-purpose flour
½ cup cornstarch
1 egg
¾ cup sparkling water
½ tsp ground turmeric
10–15 stalks of Broccolini

low-calorie oil spray
garlic aioli (bought is fine)
2 tbsp soy sauce
sesame seeds, to garnish
salt and pepper, to taste

1 Sift the flour and cornstarch into a large bowl and gradually add the egg and sparkling water, whisking all the time. Stir in the turmeric and season with salt and pepper.

2 Preheat the air fryer to 400°F for 5 minutes, then reduce the temperature to 375°F.

3 Dip the broccoli into the batter one at a time, shaking off any excess, then spray well with the low-calorie oil and air-fry for 7–8 minutes.

4 Sprinkle the fried florets with the sesame seeds, and serve with the garlic aioli and soy sauce.

The flavours here were inspired by cacio e pepe – cheese (parmesan) and black pepper – which go so well with cooked veg. When I am meal prepping this is one of my go-to veggie sides to add nutrients to a meal along with carbs and protein, but this is also great on its own or stirred through pasta.

MEDITERRANEAN VEG
WITH PARMESAN & BLACK PEPPER

SERVES 5

1 zucchini, chopped into discs
2 red onions, sliced
handful of cherry tomatoes
1 red pepper, sliced
1 eggplant, sliced
1 yellow pepper, sliced

1 tsp dried oregano
1 tsp dried parsley
1 tsp black pepper
pinch of salt
1 tbsp oil
¾ cup parmesan, grated

1 Add all the ingredients to your air fryer drawer except the parmesan.

2 Air-fry at 350°F for 10–12 minutes – if you prefer your vegetables charred, you may choose to cook these for longer.

3 For the last 2 minutes of the cooking time, sprinkle the parmesan cheese over the veg and heat it until melted and browned.

These make a great side dish but are also so delicious piled onto a piece of toast as a light lunch. The oil spray here keeps this really low in calories, but the addition of garlic mayo means you won't feel like you're missing anything.

FRIED MUSHROOMS & GARLIC MAYO

SERVES 4

1 basket of mushrooms
½ cup all-purpose flour
2 eggs, beaten
½ cup panko breadcrumbs
low-calorie oil spray
salt and pepper, to taste

Garlic mayo
4 tbsp light mayo
3 garlic cloves, grated
pinch of salt

1 Wash the mushrooms, removing any debris, then dry them with paper towels and cut them in half.

2 Put the flour mixed with a pinch of salt and pepper in a bowl, and the eggs and breadcrumbs in two separate bowls.

3 Individually dip the mushrooms into the flour, then the eggs, then roll in the breadcrumb mix to coat. Spray really well with the low-calorie oil and cook in the air fryer for 17 minutes at 350°F. Turn halfway through the cooking time, if you can, but don't shake the drawer as you'll dislodge some of the breadcrumbs.

4 Combine all the ingredients for the garlic mayo in a bowl to serve alongside the mushrooms.

If you want to keep the mushrooms whole they will need 16–18 minutes in the air fryer.

These are absolutely gorgeous, and while perfect as a light bite on their own they also go down a treat as a side dish to almost anything. Basil, garlic, lemon and chilli – what could go wrong? Personally, I could eat 10 lb of these, let alone 2 lb.

SWEET POTATO WEDGES
WITH A CHILLI, LEMON & BASIL DRESSING

SERVES 4

2 ¼ lb sweet potatoes, sliced into wedges, skin on
low-calorie spray oil
Dressing
handful of fresh basil
1 red chilli, deseeded and finely chopped

4 garlic cloves, crushed
zest and juice of 1 lemon
1 tbsp oil
pinch of salt

1 Spray the sweet potatoes with the low-calorie oil, sprinkle with salt and air-fry at 400°F for 15 minutes. Shake halfway through as sweet potato cooks quickly and can burn easily.

2 While the wedges are cooking, make the dressing by combining all the ingredients.

3 Coat the cooked wedges in the dressing.

There are so many ways to make the perfect roastie in an air fryer, one of them being to use a really low-calorie spray. You can do this if you want to reduce the calories as much as possible, but I find just adding a tiny bit of oil here really makes a difference to the taste. You can (and I do sometimes) cook these without parboiling the potatoes first, but it will mean you won't get the insides as fluffy.

AIR-FRIED 'ROAST' POTATOES
WITH FRESH ROSEMARY

SERVES 4

1 ⅓ lb potatoes, peeled and cut into chunks (I love a fingerling, but use your favourite)

2 tbsp oil or a few squirts of a low-calorie oil spray

fresh rosemary, chopped
salt and pepper, to taste

1 Parboil your potatoes for 8 minutes, then drain and give them a bit of a shake in the pot to fluff up the outsides a bit.

2 Add them to the air fryer but remove the grid at the bottom if you have one – you want them to sit in the small serving of oil. Spray the potatoes with low-calorie oil or add 2 tablespoons of oil.

3 Air-fry at 400°F for 22 minutes, but shake them after 10 minutes and again at 15 minutes. Have a snoop and spray in some more low-calorie oil, if required.

4 For the last few minutes, add in the rosemary and a sprinkle of salt and pepper.

You can save 230 total calories across the whole serving if you replace 2 tablespoons of oil with low-calorie oil spray.

These are fries taken to the next level, and I have been known to eat them with everything: burgers, curries, noodles or just on their own. I do cheat slightly on this recipe and use curry sauce; you can make your own if you prefer, or just skip it and have the fries as they are.

SALT & PEPPER FRIES
WITH CURRY SAUCE

SERVES 3

1 lb potatoes, peeled and
  chopped into fries
low-calorie oil spray
1 onion, sliced
1 red pepper, sliced
1 green pepper, sliced
spring onions, sliced

1 tsp chilli flakes
1 heaped tsp Chinese 5 spice
1 tsp garlic powder or
  chopped garlic
1 packet of curry sauce
salt and pepper, to taste

1 Put the potatoes into a bowl of cold water for 15 minutes. Drain, then pat dry with a clean tea towel.

2 In a glass or microwaveable bowl, microwave the fries for 8 minutes on high.

3 Season with a tiny pinch of salt and pepper, spray very well with the low-calorie oil, and cook in the air fryer at 400°F for 15–20 minutes (depending on how thick you cut them) until cooked through. Spraying well with a low-calorie oil is key. Shake halfway through the cooking time.

4 Around 2 minutes before the fries are ready, soften the onion, peppers and spring onions in a pan over a medium heat and toss in the spices.

5 Once the fries are cooked, add these to the pan.

6 Heat the curry sauce until piping hot. Top the fries with the curry sauce just before serving.

The first time I shared this recipe it instantly went viral. These are those gorgeous, cubed potatoes you get in a restaurant but with a low-calorie focus and, even better, no parboiling or peeling is required. Crispy, loaded with garlic and topped with some parmesan – it's a winner all round.

GARLIC & PARMESAN CRISPY CUBED POTATOES

SERVES 4

1 ½ lb baby potatoes, chopped into cubes, skin on
1 tsp paprika
1 tbsp oil

pinch of salt
½ cup light or half-fat butter
4 garlic cloves, crushed or grated
¼ cup parmesan, grated

1 Put the potatoes in a bowl with the paprika, oil and salt and turn to coat.

2 Air-fry the potatoes at 400°F for 20 minutes, shaking them three times for an even cook.

3 Finally, melt the butter in a bowl in the microwave along with the garlic – you could do this in a pan but the microwave is the quicker option. Then, in a large bowl, mix together the cooked potatoes and garlic butter, then sprinkle with the parmesan.

SWEET
TREATS

I have lost count of how many times I have made this – I'm obsessed. You can buy individual bags of chocolate-coated popcorn at the supermarket, but they are quite pricey, so here is a recipe you can make at home time and time again. (Or in my case, time and time and time again.)

WHITE CHOCOLATE-COATED POPCORN

SERVES 3

½ cup popcorn kernels
4 oz white chocolate
2 tbsp butter (I use light or half-fat butter)

1 tbsp honey
1 tsp sea salt
1½ tbsp coloured sugar sprinkles

1 Preheat the air fryer to 400°F so it is hot and ready.

2 Line your air fryer basket with some foil and add the popcorn kernels – there's no need to cover the corn with foil.

3 Air-fry at 400°F for 8–9 minutes. Once the popcorn is done, don't open the drawer for 30 seconds or so as some of the kernels might still be doing their thing.

4 While the corn is cooking, in a microwaveable bowl, melt the chocolate and butter for about two one-minute bursts. Once melted, stir in the honey and salt.

5 In a large bowl, mix together the popcorn and buttery white chocolate, then scatter over the sprinkles – you can be creative and use whatever sprinkles you like.

I dread to think just how many times I have made French toast, it's probably beyond normal, and I'm ok with that. I do change up the sauce for these – you can just use a chocolate hazelnut spread or even a berry compote instead of the speculoos if you want to take your French toast to a whole new level.

FRENCH TOAST BITES
WITH A MELTED SPECULOOS DRIZZLE

SERVES 4

1 good sourdough loaf or
   bread of your choice
2 eggs, beaten
¾ cup milk
1 tsp vanilla extract

1 tsp ground cinnamon
low-calorie oil spray
1 tbsp baker's sugar
2 tbsp smooth speculoos
   spread (I use Biscoff)

1 Cut up the sourdough or bread of choice into chunks – you can get rid of the crust if you prefer it softer.

2 Combine the eggs, milk, vanilla and cinnamon. Dip the bread chunks into the mixture to lightly coat, shake off the excess, then spray really well with the low-calorie oil and air-fry at 375°F for 6–7 minutes.

3 Once cooked, sprinkle with the sugar.

4 Melt the Biscoff spread in a microwaveable bowl in the microwave for 50–60 seconds, then drizzle over the toast bites.

SWEET TREATS

This is a gorgeous sweet treat that is perfect if you are craving something with sugar in it. The custard here is actually a fake version made using egg, yogurt and vanilla, but it tastes delicious. If you want to add extra sweetness, I sometimes top this with some chocolate chips.

FRUIT- & CUSTARD-TOPPED TOAST

SERVES 3

3 thick slices of bread
3 heaped tbsp yogurt
1 tsp vanilla extract
1 egg
handful of fresh blueberries
6 strawberries, chopped

chocolate buttons (optional)
fresh mint (pick the smaller leaves), to garnish
1 tbsp honey, to drizzle (optional)

1 Press the bread slices down in the centre with a spoon to create a dip for the fruit to sit in.

2 In a bowl, beat the yogurt, vanilla and egg then spoon a little of this mixture equally onto the slices of bread.

3 Top with the fruit and the chocolate buttons, if using.

4 Lay the bread slices flat in the air fryer and cook at 350°F for 8 minutes.

5 Top with the mint leaves and a drizzle of honey, if you like.

Calories have been calculated without the chocolate buttons or the honey drizzle but they're great additions.

PER SERVING
272
CALORIES

These yummy, crispy parcels take their inspiration from baklava, which is usually soaked in syrup and filled with chopped nuts. These filo parcels are just delicious – they do carry a high calorie count, thanks to the butter and chocolate hazelnut spread, but every bite is worth it. You can make these in a ball or folded like a samosa.

FILO PASTRY PARCELS

MAKES 8 PARCELS

⅓ cup chopped pistachios
½ cup chocolate hazelnut
    spread (I use Nutella)
pinch of sea salt

5 tbsp honey
zest of 1 lime
4 sheets of filo pastry
⅓ cup butter, melted

1 In a bowl, combine the chopped nuts, chocolate hazelnut spread, salt, honey and lime zest.

2 Unroll the 4 filo pastry sheets, then layer on top of one another. Brush every sheet with some of the melted butter and divide into 8 squares – you may need to divide larger sheets into 10.

3 Place about 1½ teaspoons of the chocolate, honey and nut mix into the middle of each filo square. Fold up the corners of the filo squares and twist the top so the parcel is sealed. You could also make into a samosa-shaped triangle. Brush the outside of each parcel with some of the melted butter.

4 Cook in the air fryer at 400°F for about 8 minutes.

5 Let them cool for a few minutes before eating, as the chocolate and honey will be piping hot.

If serving to a crowd, drizzle over some extra melted chocolate hazelnut spread and chopped pistachios.

EACH
185
CALORIES

This is more of a cheat's way of making donuts. Traditionally, they're made with yeast and deep-fried, but this is an easier, simplified version that uses far less oil. I like to get creative with my toppings and tend to use a few different options, like the glaze or sugar mix I've given below, but I also love adding a little melted chocolate if I'm feeling more indulgent. This usually makes about 8 individual donuts, but be warned you may eat more than one!

LAZY AIR-FRYER DONUTS

MAKES 8 DONUTS

1 ½ cups self-raising flour,
   plus extra for dusting
1 egg
¾ cup Greek yogurt
1 tsp vanilla extract
1 tsp granulated sweetener
   (optional)
low-calorie oil spray

Coating (optional)
⅔ cup icing sugar
3 tbsp skim milk
1 tsp ground cinnamon
2 tbsp sugar
3 tbsp melted half-fat butter

These are also really fun dipped in coloured sprinkles, just follow the method for the coating and use sprinkles instead of the cinnamon/sugar mix.

1 In a bowl, mix together the flour, egg, yogurt, vanilla and sweetener and form into a dough.

2 On a floured surface, divide the dough into 4, then roll each piece into long, thin, sausages. Cut along the length to give you two long pieces and form each piece into a ring.

3 Spray your air fryer tray with a low-calorie oil or line it with baking parchment, then preheat your air fryer so the donuts instantly hit the heat.

4 Spray the donuts well with a low-calorie oil and air-fry at 400°F for 7 minutes, flipping them halfway through cooking.

5 If you want to top the donuts, either combine the icing sugar and milk to create a glaze and pour it over the donuts, or combine the cinnamon and sugar in a bowl, dip the top of each donut into the melted butter, then into the sugar mix to coat.

This is so easy I am not sure I can even call this a recipe – with just three ingredients. This is one for those with a serious sweet tooth. When I first posted this dish on social media it went viral on an entirely new scale for me – it was featured in national newspapers and even made it onto an American TV news channel! Feel free to be creative with your choice of chocolate egg and if you can't get the croissant roll, just use puff pastry.

CHOCOLATE EGG CROISSANT BALLS

MAKES 6

6 chocolate eggs (I use
   Cadbury Creme Eggs)
1 packet of croissant
   pastry (find these in the
   refrigerated aisle with
   the pastry)
1 egg, beaten

1 Wrap each chocolate egg in a strip of pastry so it is completely covered. Roll and shape the pastry so it is a ball and fully closed.

2 Brush with the beaten egg, then air-fry at 350°F for 8 minutes.

I am obsessed with this, it takes hardly any prep and whether you want it as a dessert for a dinner party or just a sweet treat for yourself, this is the one. These are a low-calorie alternative to rich desserts and will definitely satisfy that sweet craving.

PEACHES
WITH ICE CREAM, HONEY & PISTACHIOS

SERVES 4

4 tbsp honey, plus extra for drizzling
1 heaped tsp ground cinnamon
2 fresh peaches, halved and stoned
low-calorie oil spray

ice cream of your choice (use a low-calorie alternative or frozen yogurt)
handful of chopped pistachios
fresh mint leaves

1 In a bowl, combine the honey and cinnamon.

2 Spray the peach halves with low-calorie oil and cook in the air fryer at 335°F for 5 minutes. After 5 minutes, spoon over the honey and cinnamon mix, then cook for another 8 minutes – you can just add this at the start, but it might caramelise too much and burn slightly.

3 Let the peaches cool for 2 minutes, then serve with ice cream, pistachios, mint and an extra drizzle of honey, if you fancy.

So, I love cookies, but I don't like making a batch and then either having to eat or freeze them all. (I have a small freezer so I try to plan what I'm going to fill it up with.) Sometimes, you're in the mood for just *one* cookie, and this is an amazing one for just such an occasion. This cookie is quite large, so in theory should serve two people with a nice cuppa. I have had it all to myself on occasions, though, so don't feel like you NEED to share...

GIANT COOKIE

SERVES 2

½ cup all-purpose flour
¼ tsp baking soda
pinch of sea salt
3 tbsp melted light butter
5 tbsp brown sugar
1 large egg

¾ tsp vanilla extract
good handful of white
 chocolate chips
handful of chopped nuts
 (I used macadamia)

1 In a bowl combine the flour, bicarbonate of soda and salt.

2 In a separate bowl, combine the melted butter and brown sugar, then stir in the egg with a spatula. Add to the flour mix and stir until a cookie dough forms, then add the white chocolate chips and nuts.

3 Shape the cookie into one large ball and place on some baking parchment in your air fryer. Cook at 160°C for 12–13 minutes.

4 To get that ultra perfect cookie pie shape, if your air fryer has capacity, add the cookie to a 6-in cake tin.

SWEET TREATS

INDEX

ACKNOWLEDGEMENTS

To Mum and Dad who I love even more than my air fryer (it was a close call though). To Lizzy & Celia for seeing the potential in Bored of Lunch as a book. Finally, to my AMAZING online community of lunchers without whose support, I wouldn't be writing cookbooks. Thank you!

Text © Nathan Anthony 2023
Photography © Clare Wilkinson 2023

Nathan Anthony has asserted his right to be identified
as the author of this Work in accordance with the
Copyright, Designs and Patents Act 1988

Photography: Clare Wilkinson
Food and prop styling: Charlotte O'Connell
Styling assistant: Susan Willis
Design: maru studio

Sourcebooks and the colophon are registered
trademarks of Sourcebooks.

Published by Sourcebooks
P.O. Box 4410, Naperville, Illinois 60567-4410
(630) 961-3900
sourcebooks.com

Originally published in 2023 in Great Britain by Ebury Press,
an imprint of Ebury Publishing. Ebury Press is part of the
Penguin Random House group of companies whose addresses
can be found at global.penguinrandomhouse.com

Cataloging-in-Publication Data is on file
with the Library of Congress.

Printed and bound in Vietnam.
EBY 10 9 8 7 6 5 4 3 2 1

This book is made from Forest Stewardship Council® certified paper.